BALTIC
JEWELS

JILL RICHARDSON FOLLOWED ANCIENT EXPLORERS AND MEDIEVAL
TRADERS INTO THE BALTIC — AND RETURNED WITH TREASURES

Somehow I had expected the Baltic to take itself more seriously – after all, it is a great historic trading route. But now, whenever I think about it, it comes to mind in an explosion of colour. Tall painted houses in Stockholm and Copenhagen; the red-tiled roofs and copper-green spires of Tallinn's skyline; displays of amber in Poland; the treasures of the Hermitage in St Petersburg. And sunshine, glittering on gilded domes and splashing on the sea.

Actually, my sunglasses seemed to be on permanent duty, as I found myself gazing at the views from our ship. Countless islands captivated me as I leant on the railings in the warm summer weather, watching panoramas slip by from my own peaceful balcony.

There's no better way of exploring the Baltic countries than on a cruise: for centuries this sea has been their highway. I loved the sense of history evoked by sea travel. Capitals such as Copenhagen and Tallinn face the water, welcoming us as they have welcomed visitors for generations. Well, perhaps visitors were not always greeted as kindly as we were: such was Tallinn's strategic importance that for 700 years successive waves of Danes, Germans, Swedes and Russians played pass-the-parcel with it.

Taking a fly-cruise from Copenhagen meant I wasted no time travelling to the Baltic and could spend my whole holiday exploring. In 2004 Grand Princess will be the largest cruise ship in the region.

▹ ▹ ▹ ▹ ▹ ▹ ▹ ▹ ▹ ▹ ▹

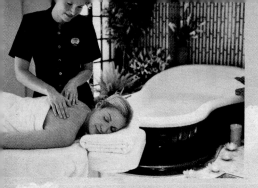

Before we even set sail, I realised there was only one pace of life-my own. Having planned for – and missed – the morning aerobics class, I found that the super-sleek gym, with its sea views, was just as fun...and afterwards discovered the magic of a hot stone massage. The Princess lifestyle is like that: you can fill every moment with activity or take an active decision to do nothing but watch the world go by.

Princess, P&O Cruises' American sister line, has taken the best principles of cruising and re-mixed them here with 21st-century style and innovation. So you can find an intimate piano bar or enjoy late-night jazz, but there's also Skywalkers nightclub suspended spaceship-like 150 feet above the waves.

Wherever you wander, there is choice – a library and an internet café; Broadway-style shows or live sports on television. With dining too, Princess does more than any other cruise line, offering traditional fixed seating if you like to eat with the same people and get to know your waiter, or 'anytime' dining where you can ring the changes. The three main dining rooms serve delectable

meals but I also liked the option of scuttling off for a grill or an Italian feast in Sabatini's Trattoria. You get all the pampering that you'd expect from a cruise plus Princess's 'no problem' American service standards.

From the moment I caught sight of the Little Mermaid statue in front of Copenhagen's Citadel, I felt a thrill: suddenly life was being breathed into the guidebook pictures. Visiting all the Scandinavian capitals together was fascinating because they are so different from one another. Stockholm, amid its own archipelago, is one-third water and one-third parkland. You can explore both on the island of Djurgården, a former hunting ground in the heart of the city. It is also home to the Vasa Museum. Vasa, a royal warship, sank on her maiden voyage in 1628. Raised in 1961, she is now a fabulous vision of the 17th century.

The open-air museums in Stockholm and Oslo are both wonderful, whisking you back in time. Helsinki has a clean, contemporary feel but its Suomenlinna Sea Fortress – a World Heritage Site – speaks of its history. Another World Heritage Site lies just across the water: Tallinn's

Old Town, still wrapped in much of its great medieval wall, with cobbled streets and charming squares.

Our cruise's climax was two glorious days in the city of the tsars, St Petersburg – home to the Hermitage, one of the world's greatest art museums. Here I was dazzled by Etruscan vases, Roman statues and treasuries of gold, but also by masterpieces by da Vinci, Rembrandt and the Impressionists. I left overwhelmed by how much remained to seen – some three million exhibits.

Nor is the Hermitage all: St Petersburg is ringed with imperial palaces and gardens, studded with gorgeous onion-domed cathedrals and threaded with tranquil canals. Peterhof – a Russian Versailles with hundreds of ornate fountains – was worth every minute of the journey out of town but, back in the city, another memory of its founder, Peter the Great was more touching: his first home there – a simple wooden cottage.

Images, memories... brilliant treasures from the Baltic.

PRINCESS CRUISES

Cruise the Baltic – save up to 40%

10-night Baltic Jewels#

Day 1	Fly UK/Copenhagen - embark Grand Princess
Day 2	At sea
Day 3	Stockholm
Day 4	Helsinki
Day 5	St Petersburg - overnight
Day 6	St Petersburg
Day 7	Tallinn
Day 8	Gdansk
Day 9	At sea
Day 10	Oslo
Day 11	Copenhagen - disembark and fly home

The holiday featured on these pages is Princess Cruises' 10-night Baltic Jewels departing from May '04 - Aug '04. Prices start from £1,169* per person, including up to 40% discount, return flights from London, transfers plus accommodation, meals and entertainment onboard Grand Princess if you book by 29 February '04.

To order your brochure complete and return the attached coupon, visit your ABTA travel agent or call our brochure request line: **0870 242 0100** quoting reference RD2.

JOHN BLAIS

[features]

[departments]

27
Test your knowlege of all words Celtic

DAVE KLUG

33 Meeting a boy from Peru gave Elaine Paige a new perspective

151 RDLiving
NEWS, ADVICE, FACTS, FUN

152 Health Winter cough? Look out for these danger signs! Plus managing your migraine, losing weight in 2,000 easy steps and why mums-to-be must brush their teeth carefully

156 Food How to ease a partied-out liver, finding the freshest fish and bad news about cola

158 You An expert guide to winning arguments, keeping New Year resolutions and those rituals that could save your marriage

160 Technology A phone-controlled car, faxing without a fax machine and the truth about downloading music

162 Money Your rights when returning goods, a handy way to stay fully insured and where to shop for Fair Trade goods

153
Hobbies that heal

CHIP SIMONS/TAXI/GETTY IMAGES

| Health | Travel | At Home | Laughfinder | Word Power | Shopping Digest |

For these features and more, click on ▶ | **THIS MONTH'S ISSUE**

TIMOTHY WHITE/CORBIS OUTLINE

Pretty Woman

Interested in Hollywood's hottest female star? In our feature on page 68, Julia Roberts talks frankly about marriage, gossip columnists and her pet geese. Log on to www.readersdigest.co.uk for a link to a preview of her latest movie, *Mona Lisa Smile*

TESTING THE WATER

Kidney disease is a silent killer in Britain (see page 113). As many as a quarter of a million of us may have some form of kidney disease without knowing it.

Wellbeing MET has produced an easy at-home test kit to detect the early warning signs of kidney disease by measuring the presence of protein in the urine.

This potentially life-saving test is available at a special price for Reader's Digest readers.

Visit our website for further details, and for links to specialist resources for kidney patients

Self Assessment Test Kit - for kidney disease - 2 tests for home use

Online Favourites

- ▶ **PLAY** interactive Word Power
- ▶ **VISIT** our Laughfinder for jokes on everything... and anything (and you get to rate them too)
- ▶ **TRY** our recipe of the day
- ▶ **BROWSE** through Shopping Digest and see the winners of our famous Prize Draw

Banishing Bashfulness

Many of us suffer from anxiety in social situations that prevents us from living our lives to the full (see page 124). For more information on how to combat shyness visit www.readersdigest.co.uk

The swinging sixties? Those Were The Days My Friend.

Nowadays, you can look forward to some great days out thanks to a Senior Railcard.
It saves you 1/3 on most rail fares throughout Britain,
and costs just £18 a year, which you could recoup in one journey.

So, pop down to your nearest staffed train station and pick up a leaflet today or phone
08457 48 49 50 and ask for the telesales number of your nearest Train Company.

National Rail   www.senior-railcard.co.uk

Reader's Digest

BRITAIN'S BEST-SELLING MONTHLY MAGAZINE JANUARY 2004 NO 981

Editor-in-Chief Katherine Walker
Features Editor Tim Bouquet
Senior Editors Tricia Mallett, Simon Hartley
Research Editor Lucy Wildman
Production Editor Catherine Haughney
Excerpts Editor Lisa Loveday
Sub-Editors Simon Hemelryk, Lorraine Thompson
Assistant Excerpts Editor Andrew Morris
Deputy Research Editors Lucy Baylis,
Catherine Farror
Magazine Administrator Joanna Cruddas
Editorial Secretary Nina Sadgrove
Design Director Martin Colyer
Picture Researcher Donna Clews

European Research Editor Lisa Donafee

Advertisement Director Flora MacMillan
Advertising Sales Managers Hayley Green,
Sharon Jupp, Jayne Ross, Samantha Scattergood,
Jennifer Schultes, Simon Tucker

Director Circulation Wendy Sly
Research Manager Suzanne Lugthart
Senior Production Controller Sandra Dixon-May
Customer Service Manager Justin Webster
Publisher Victoria Scott
Managing Director Andrew Lynam-Smith
Directors Peter Brady, Martin Pasteiner,
Andrew Wilton

READER'S DIGEST ASSOCIATION, INC
Founders DeWitt Wallace and Lila Acheson Wallace
Chairman, Chief Executive Officer Thomas O. Ryder
Editor-in-Chief Eric W. Schrier
President, International Thomas D. Gardner
Editorial Director, International Conrad Kiechel

**Reader's Digest is published in
48 editions in 19 languages**

HOW TO REACH US

Letters to the Editor
● theeditor@readersdigest.co.uk

You Said It
● YouSaidIt@readersdigest.co.uk
● You Said It, Reader's Digest,
11 Westferry Circus, London E14 4HE.
This address is also correct for
submissions to **Local Heroes**. Mark
your envelope appropriately. Include your
first name and surname, address,
e-mail and daytime phone number with
all correspondence.
  We may edit letters, and use them in all
print and electronic media.

Subscriptions
● www.readersdigest.co.uk
● Reader's Digest Association, Freepost,
NAT3782, Leicester LE55 8BA.
UK £42 a year. Republic of Ireland
€74.39 a year. Europe £50 a year. Rest of the
world £60 a year. Prices include delivery.

Customer Services
Check your account, pay a bill, change
your address and browse our online
shop at www.readersdigest.co.uk
● 08705 113366
● cust_service@readersdigest.co.uk
● minicom: 01502 502664

Moving?
● www.readersdigest.co.uk
● 08705 113366

Submissions
For short humour items, see page 13.
We cannot accept or acknowledge
unsolicited article-length manuscripts.

IT'S A FUNNY OLD WORLD

DO YOU WANT to make us laugh *and* make some money? Iain MacPherson from Thornton in Lancashire did. His true story about a fortune teller who didn't plan ahead features in All in a Day's Work on page 37. Now Iain's just a little bit richer.

If you've been involved in a funny incident or know a great joke, write and tell us about it. If we publish it, you'll have a cheque in the post to smile about. Here's what we want you to do:

YOU TELL US A STORY

that's true, not previously published and sheds light on adult human nature. And funny enough to stand out from the hundreds we get each week

WE PAY YOU £100

if we print it in **Life's Like That** or **All in a Day's Work**. We also pay £60 for contributions to **Laughter, the Best Medicine** and end-of-article fillers

THE SMALL PRINT

With all submissions, please include your full name, address and daytime phone number. We cannot acknowledge or return items we do not publish. Article-length stories, poetry and cartoons are not requested. Contributions used become world copyright of the Reader's Digest Association Limited

HOW TO SUBMIT

- Write to Excerpts at: Reader's Digest, 11 Westferry Circus, London E14 4HE
- By e-mail: excerpts@readersdigest.co.uk
- Visit readersdigest.co.uk. Click on "We pay for your story"

New Energy

CONGRATULATIONS on a fine article debunking the monstrosities that are ruining not only our countryside, but the health of people forced to live by them ("Tilting Against Windmills").

Most of the companies developing wind farms are multinationals racing to a honeypot of profit. Why is the Government giving them so much support, especially given most engineering societies are against turbines on the grounds of efficiency?

KEITH FAICHNEY, Lancaster

If the Government's target of 20 per cent of electricity generation from renewable sources by 2020 were met by wind energy, this would mean installing two turbines a day for the next 18 years. There are many other means of sustainable energy power, such as geothermal, solar, tidal and hydro. I despair of any imaginative long-term policy from politicians.

CLIVE PRICE, London SW19

Reader's Digest published a piece on solar power last year; as a result I am having solar panels fitted. The company estimates they will produce over 80 per cent of my electricity—*and* they're not a blot on the landscape.

DIANNE HUTCHENS, Welling, Kent

Renewable energy from windmills will make a great contribution to the reduction of carbon dioxide emissions.

We are at a turning point. We can continue in the old way and wreck the planet or invest in new technology that will provide electricity and leave a habitable world for our children.

IRENE WILLIS, Canvey Island, Essex

School Assessment

IN RESPONSE TO the letter from Charles Clarke, Secretary of State for Education and Skills ("You Said It"), in which he said that "without tests at seven, 11 and 14, it is impossible to see how a child is doing", I would like to ask whether he has any idea how insulting he is being to the teaching profession.

As a primary school teacher, I mark, level and moderate children's work on a daily basis; the day that a SAT result tells me something I didn't already know is the day I should stop teaching. If he really believes this,

15

there is less hope than I thought for an increasingly struggling system.

CATHY FARMER, Bude, Cornwall

Capsule Confusion

AFTER READING about mercury levels in fish ("Hidden Dangers in 'Healthy' Foods"), I am now wondering about taking fish-oil supplements.

It would be helpful if this was clarified. KENNETH O'CONNOR, Sutton, Surrey

Diane Benford, a senior toxicologist at the Food Standards Agency, says, "Mercury in fish is mainly in the flesh and very little of it passes into fish oil." A Government survey showed mercury levels in a number of fish-oil based supplements were very low and in many cases mercury was not detected. EDS

Unhealthy State

IT REALLY IS TIME the Government got a grip of the problem highlighted in "Why Are These Doctors Paid to Sit at Home".

There should be an independent investigation of all current suspensions of more than two weeks. Any found to be unjustified or retaliatory should result in the doctor's reinstatement and a written warning for the manager concerned. RICHARD ASLIN, Burnley

Having worked in the NHS, I have seen much of what you wrote about, especially bullying. Statistics show that over one third of NHS staff are bullied,

'Thompson gets great results, despite his lack of people skills'

many of whom say nothing as they are scared of losing their job. As a result, good people leave and bad ones stay in the system. MARIE-CLAIRE OLIVER, Bath

Inspired Service

JAMIE OLIVER'S piece "He Taught Me Passion" (October) reminded me of an episode when I was 20.

I was alone on holiday in London. I'd just had a pizza, but my wanderings took me into Soho and I suddenly wanted a "sophisticated" meal.

So I entered Gennaro Contaldo's restaurant and ordered two courses; by the time the main course arrived, I deeply regretted my earlier snack.

The waiter could not have been kinder; he suggested I had a rest. He was sympathetic and did not make me feel embarrassed.

The restaurant did for me what Gennaro himself did for Oliver— showed me "sensitivity and common sense". L. P. HEDGES, Blackpool

The magic of NEW ZEALAND

27 day Escorted Tour   from **£2,595**

On an All Ways Pacific Escorted Tour you will find yourself with a group of like-minded travellers who really want to get close to the people, culture and natural wonders of New Zealand.

Our planning is meticulous and our dedication to client service is second to none. Every hotel is personally selected for your comfort, every road for its scenic beauty and every location for its interest and experiences, to make this the holiday of a lifetime.

Bay of Islands
to Heathrow
Auckland
Rotorua
Napier
from Singapore
Picton
Wellington
Greymouth
Kaikaura
Glaciers
Haast
Christchurch
Mt Cook
Milford Sound
Queenstown
Te Anau
Dunedin

YOUR ITINERARY:

2 Nights	**Singapore**
2 Nights	**Christchurch**
1 Night	**The Glaciers**
3 Nights	**Queenstown**
2 Nights	**Te Anau**
1 Night	**Dunedin**
1 Night	**Mt Cook**
1 Night	**Kaikaura**
2 Nights	**Wellington**
1 Night	**Napier**
2 Nights	**Rotorua**
3 Nights	**Bay Of Islands**
2 Nights	**Auckland**

DEPARTURE DATES 2004

06 March	£3,095	20 March	£2,995
03 April	£2,895	17 April	£2,895
08 May	£2,595	15 Oct	£2,595
29 Oct	£2,995	12 Nov	£3,095
26 Nov	£3,095	09 Dec	£3,595

DEPARTURE DATES 2005

07, 14, 21, 25, 28 Jan	£3,595
01, 04, 08, 11, 18 Feb	£3,595
25 Feb, 04, 11, 25 Mar	£3,495
08 April, 06 May	£2,995

Flights: Economy Class with Singapore Airlines. Upgrades available.
Touring: All our coaches are the most luxurious available, with panoramic windows, air conditioning and toilets. Our Coach Captain/Drivers are the best in the country.
Accommodation: in good quality hotels, all rooms with private facilities.
Meals: Full breakfast every day and most evening meals in New Zealand are included.

STOPOVERS AND EXTENSIONS
If you want to extend your stay we can arrange exciting packages and stop over options to add an extra dimension to your holiday.

All our staff have travelled extensively in the Pacific region, so call us now for more details and our Escorted Tours Brochure:

01494 432747

or clip the coupon and send it to:
All Ways Pacific Travel
7 Whielden Street
Old Amersham, Bucks HP7 0HT

ALL  WAYS
PACIFIC

ABTA V3991

Email: sales@all-ways.co.uk
Website: www.all-ways.co.uk

3485 IATA PROTECTED

BE GUIDED BY THE EXPERTS

Please send a brochure to:

Name _____

Address _____

_____

Post code _____

All Ways Pacific Travel, 7 Whielden Street
Old Amersham, Bucks HP7 0HT   RDJAN04

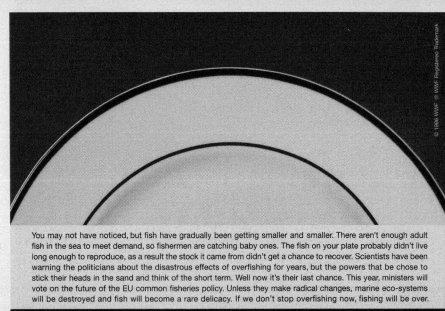

© 1986 WWF ® WWF Registered Trademark

You may not have noticed, but fish have gradually been getting smaller and smaller. There aren't enough adult fish in the sea to meet demand, so fishermen are catching baby ones. The fish on your plate probably didn't live long enough to reproduce, as a result the stock it came from didn't get a chance to recover. Scientists have been warning the politicians about the disastrous effects of overfishing for years, but the powers that be chose to stick their heads in the sand and think of the short term. Well now it's their last chance. This year, ministers will vote on the future of the EU common fisheries policy. Unless they make radical changes, marine eco-systems will be destroyed and fish will become a rare delicacy. If we don't stop overfishing now, fishing will be over.

Politicians will probably tell you that plates are getting bigger.

WWF®

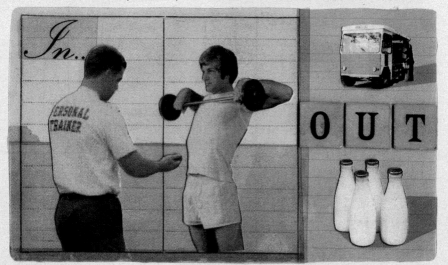

Want a 21st Century Job?

I F YOU'RE looking for career guidance, the future's in fitness, flying and fake breasts. Vocational-exams board City & Guilds has compiled a guide to which British jobs will be on the way up and which will be on the way out by 2010.

Increased affluence and shortage of time means that time-management consultants, personal trainers and plastic surgeons will be hot careers, but it's bad news for postmen (blame e-mail), milkmen (blame supermarkets), clerical jobs (blame computers) and farm workers (blame imports). We'll see more "fun employees"— whose ominous-sounding role it is to keep stressed workforces happy *and* productive—and more pilots, thanks to cheaper air fares.

If all this change makes you feel insecure, there is a positive. Estate agents and car salesmen may end up on the scrapheap as Internet-selling does their job for them.

fast fact

Happiest days. Fewer British pupils feel isolated at school than in any other developed nation

Organisation for Economic Co-operation and Development

ILLUSTRATED BY MARTIN O'NEILL

IN GOD WE JEST

Reverend Roly Bain preaches on the trials of keeping to your faith (can you spot the metaphor?) at St Albans cathedral, Herts. Roly is part of Holy Fools, a group that uses clowning to spread the Christian message

THE RD HIT LIST

We're obsessed by animals in this country. Judging by some of the 1,509,317 calls the RSPCA gets every year, our concern may be going too far:

- An inspector was called out to collect an "injured magpie" on a motorway. It was, in fact, a black-and-white Nike trainer.

- A caller thought she saw a stray cat on her bedroom floor. It was a pair of her knickers.

- Attempts to capture a black snake hiding under a settee were made easier when it was discovered the sinister creature was actually TV cables.

- A woman was made a prisoner in her own home for 24 hours by a black cat-like creature crouched on her doorstep. "Could it be the beast of Bodmin?" she asked. No, it was telephone directories in a black plastic bag.

- A common call concerns a bird trapped behind a wall. It usually turns out to be the smoke alarm bleeping because the battery is low.

ANTHONY BLAKE PICTURE LIBRARY; CHRIS YOUNG/PA

Popping Out for an English

INDIAN CURRY may be the new national dish, but the Sunday roast is fighting back, playing its Asian rival at its own game. The Three Tuns pub in Heddon, Northumberland, has started a takeaway Sunday lunch service and customers are flocking from all over the area for their meat-and-two-veg-to-go, priced £4.25. You can even have gravy, says chef Ann Ling, but you'll need to bring a flask.

A Coffin for Coughing

THE ENTRANCE to the office of Connectpoint in Manchester is sheltered from the weather, making it a mecca for office workers on fag breaks. Bosses at the advertising and PR firm thought the clouds of smoke and dog ends created a bad image, so they created a special smoking booth—a coffin tastefully lined in the Silk Cut colours with a health warning above. Creative director Simon Broadbent says his company didn't want to offend anyone, but hoped the message had got through.

GRASS ROOTS

Hard Labour of Love

TWO YEARS AGO, 39 Chapel Street, Blackpool, was a derelict eyesore, used as a crack den. Now, thanks to another gang of criminals, the ten-bedroom property is a hotel offering free holidays to terminally ill children.

The project was the last wish of Donna Curtis, a local teenager who died of leukaemia in 1996. She wanted it to be "as good as Disneyland, if not better", says her father Len, the driving force behind it. Rather than use professional builders, he enlisted a group of offenders on community service orders. They had no choice about getting involved—but became so inspired they voluntarily put in hundreds of hours of extra work.

Three of the men still work at the house, while others now have jobs in the building industry. Trevor Hall, 50, a welder convicted of fighting in a pub, has become the "in-house engineer". "Clearing that hotel was the hardest work I've ever done, but it was worth it," he says. "I'd throw a tantrum if I wasn't sent there each week."

Donna's Dreamhouse (pictured) is now a riot of Disney-themed decorations, featuring life-sized characters and a working model railway at ceiling height. One mother,

who stayed at the hotel with her daughter who suffers from cerebral palsy, was impressed: "Putting people in prison isn't benefiting anybody—this is a fabulous idea."

'There's a Child on the Ledge!'

BY LISA LOVEDAY

Paul and Adil grabbed the ladder from their van when they saw a flat on fire

O N A SWELTERING day last summer, central heating engineers Adil Sarwar and Paul Hudson were driving through a quiet suburb of Bolton, Greater Manchester, in their white Mercedes van.

They'd finished work at Amara Plumbing, the firm owned by Adil, 31, and named after his little daughter.

Paul was driving, but as the pair chatted the 39-year-old missed the usual turning for Adil's home. Instead he joined the busy main road that links Bolton to Wigan, lined either side by large terraced houses and shops with flats above.

Suddenly Paul's view ahead was obscured by smoke. "Is that a skip burning?" Adil asked. As they drew closer they saw the black columns were pouring from a first-floor flat.

"Look!" Paul said. "There's a child on the window ledge!"

A tiny Asian boy, dressed only in shorts, was huddled just above the narrow casing for the shuttering of the shop below. His small body was engulfed in smoke from the windows behind him. A crowd had gathered, ominously still. *Where are the emergency services?* Adil wondered.

The boy was swaying back and forth, as if deciding to jump—but it was too far down.

Paul slammed on his brakes. "We've got to get him down," he shouted. The two men leapt out of the van. Paul flung open the rear

PHOTOGRAPHED BY SIMON ROBERTS

23

doors, reached inside and yanked at the ropes securing their ladders. The knots were stubborn. Just as he began to panic they fell free. The men grabbed an extending ladder and sprinted across the street. Paul

The boy gazed down—
too terrified to call for help

and Adil had worked here before and they knew there were gas meters at the front of the buildings which could explode. The boy gazed down at them, too terrified to call for help.

Hitching their ladder up the front of the shop, Adil sprang upwards, Paul a few rungs behind. They knew it was dangerous having two men on a ladder, but getting the boy fast was a two-man job. Adil swung his right foot on to the narrow ledge, hooked his left arm around the frame of an open window to stop himself falling, and stretched out towards the boy.

Grasping the child's fingers, he pulled him inch by inch towards Paul, now positioned at the top of the ladder. Paul took the boy in his arms and gingerly climbed down the rungs. High up on the ledge, Adil

WANTED: YOUR HEROES!

Do you know someone who inspires you? If so, please write to us. We pay £100 for published contributions. Your nominee could feature on our back cover. Send details to the address on page 10.

realised the fire was out of control. Thick, noxious smoke gushed from every opening, seeped from tiny gaps and fissures. But as a father, he knew he had to check if any of the boy's family were trapped inside. He took a deep breath and jumped in through the open window.

A wall of smoke rising through the floorboards blinded him. Groping, Adil felt twin beds on either side of the window. He searched with his palms underneath them, pulled back the covers. *No bodies.* Where next?

The temperature was soaring, but Adil was oblivious to heat and time. Unable to hold his breath any longer, he inhaled. Fumes rasped his lungs.

"The family's out! Get out!" It was Paul shouting from the ladder.

Coughing violently, eyes streaming, Adil retreated to the window. When he got back on the ground, five-year-old Ilyas Mogradia had been reunited with his parents and three siblings who had escaped via a back door, the only exit.

The road was now swarming with fire engines, ambulances and police. Quietly Adil and Paul took their ladder back to the van and drove off. Their identities were only revealed after a colleague rang the local paper and reported their bravery, all down to taking a wrong turn.

"If you see a child who needs help, you just go over and help," says Adil, now recovered from smoke inhalation. "It was just about doing the right thing."

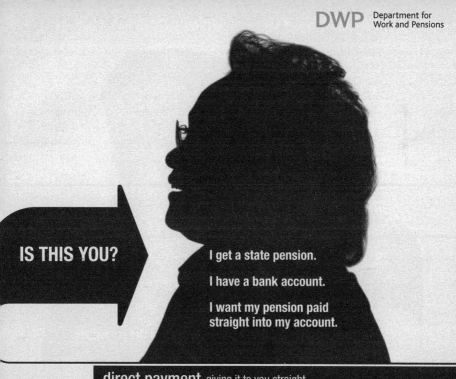

DWP Department for Work and Pensions

IS THIS YOU?

I get a state pension.

I have a bank account.

I want my pension paid straight into my account.

direct payment giving it to you straight

If you agree with the statements above, it's easy to get what you want from Direct Payment.

All we need are your account details.

- Wait for your Direct Payment letter and leaflet.
- Fill in the form with your account details.
- Return your form, free.
- Wait for your letter telling you when your first payment will be made.

Job done.

For more information call **0800 107 2000**
(textphone 0800 107 4000 if you have hearing or speech difficulties).
Lines open 8am to 9pm weekdays, 9am to 5pm weekends.

www.dwp.gov.uk/directpayment

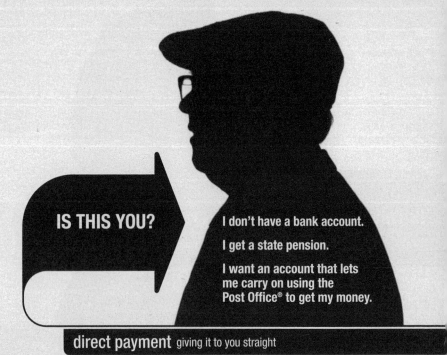

IS THIS YOU?

I don't have a bank account.

I get a state pension.

I want an account that lets me carry on using the Post Office® to get my money.

direct payment giving it to you straight

If you agree with the statements above, Direct Payment can help you to get what you want.

- There are lots of accounts that give you the option of using the Post Office®.

- There are current accounts and basic bank accounts from some banks and building societies, and the Post Office® card account.

- To find out more about accounts with Post Office® access, call the number below.

There, clear as a bell.

For more information call **0800 107 2000**
(textphone 0800 107 4000 if you have hearing or speech difficulties).
Lines open 8am to 9pm weekdays, 9am to 5pm weekends

www.dwp.gov.uk/directpayment

WORD POWER

Slàinte! (SLAWN-chuh!) That's a toast to your health from us to you for the New Year. The number of Gaelic speakers in Scotland is in decline, according to the last census. Time then, in the month when we celebrate Burns' Night, to remember how much the Celts of Scotland, Ireland and Wales have contributed to the English language. Answers are on the next page.

1 **keen** *v*—A: to sail. B: shout. C: giggle. D: wail.

2 **smidgen** *n*—A: smear of mud or dirt. B: short person. C: small amount. D: tiny dove.

3 **bard** *n*—one who A: is excluded. B: is angry. C: rides horses. D: writes poetry.

4 **cairn** *n*—A: alligator. B: pile of stones. C: spinning wheel. D: statue.

5 **smithereens** *n*—A: deep valleys. B: particles of dirt. C: silver pitchers. D: small pieces.

6 **dinky** *adj*—A: neat. B: generous. C: mean. D: dull and boring.

7 **galore** *adv*—A: in excess. B: in an awkward manner. C: in plentiful amounts. D: in an elegant way.

8 **brogue** *n*—A: dishonest person. B: shoe. C: elaborate needlework. D: foreign language.

9 **blather** *v*—A: to annoy. B: wash. C: stutter. D: talk foolishly.

10 **slew** *n*—A: large number. B: hunter's kill. C: horse-drawn carriage. D: chimney air duct.

11 **hooligan** *n*—A: thug. B: tin whistle player. C: commotion. D: street gang.

12 **slogan** *n*—A: long walk. B: untidy person. C: distinctive phrase. D: rhyming song.

13 **caddie** *n*—person who A: makes the tea in a hotel. B: delivers newspapers. C: takes care of other people's horses. D: carries a golfer's clubs.

14 **duffer** *n*—A: master of ceremonies. B: type of fabric. C: incompetent person. D: kind of pastry.

15 **gumption** *n*—A: elbow grease. B: resourcefulness. C: lineament. D: bad manners.

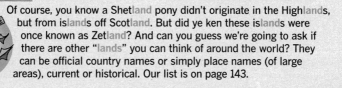

Of course, you know a Shetland pony didn't originate in the Highlands, but from islands off Scotland. But did ye ken these islands were once known as Zetland? And can you guess we're going to ask if there are other "lands" you can think of around the world? They can be official country names or simply place names (of large areas), current or historical. Our list is on page 143.

ILLUSTRATED BY DAVE KLUG

ANSWERS:

1 **keen**—*[D]* To wail in lament for the dead. "While the bagpipes played, the *keening* widow was led from the church." Irish *caoinim* (I wail).

2 **smidgen**—*[C]* A small amount. "The photographer asked the girl to move a *smidgen* to the left." Nineteenth century English, perhaps from Scots *smitch* (small amount or insignificant person).

3 **bard**—*[D]* A poet, traditionally one who wrote and recited epic poems. *From Scottish Gaelic *bàrd*, Irish *bard*, Welsh *bardd*.

4 **cairn**—*[B]* A pile of stones set up as a monument or landmark or prehistoric burial mound. Scottish Gaelic.

5 **smithereens**—*[D]* Small pieces. "The mirror was broken into *smithereens*." Irish *smidirín*.

6 **dinky**—*[A]* Small and neat; cute. "She had an old cottage with a *dinky* garden." Scots and northern English dialect *dink* (neat, trim).

7 **galore**—*[C]* In plentiful amounts. "The victory was celebrated with food and drink *galore*." Irish *go leor*, (to sufficiency).

8 **brogue**—*[B]* Sturdy shoe worn in Ireland and the Scottish Highlands; also, a strong accent in the pronunciation of English by Irish or Scottish people. Scottish Gaelic and Irish *bróg* (shoe).

9 **blather**—*[D]* To talk foolishly or babble without making much sense. "He *blathered* on, making feeble excuses." Scots and northern English dialect from Old Norse *blathra* (to talk nonsense).

10 **slew**—*[A]* A large number or quantity. "A *slew* of people waited for the mayor-elect to arrive." Irish *sluagh*.

11 **hooligan**—*[A]* A young thug or street hoodlum. From the Irish surname of a fictional rowdy family who featured in a popular 1890s music-hall song.

12 **slogan**—*[C]* A distinctive phrase often associated with a political party or product. " 'Go to work on an egg' was a familiar advertising *slogan* of the Sixties." Also a Scottish Highland war cry. Gaelic *sluagh* (army) and *ghairm* (shout).

13 **caddie**—*[D]* A person who carries a golfer's clubs. "The *caddie* managed to sell his memoirs when he retired." Scots (a gentleman who joined the army without a commission).

14 **duffer**—*[C]* An incompetent or slow-witted person. "He was a complete *duffer* when it came to using a computer." Scots *dowfart* (stupid person).

15 **gumption**—*[B]* Resourcefulness of a shrewd or spirited kind. "At least she had the *gumption* to get advice from an expert." Scots.

*In a few cases, the only difference between the Scots and Irish word is an accent mark.

VOCABULARY RATINGS
15-14 Excellent **13-12** Good **11-9** Fair

Is this the most important thing you will read today?

It may surprise you to know that bowel cancer is the second most common cause of cancer death in the UK. One reason for this is the embarrassment and fear surrounding the disease, which means that people often do not act upon their symptoms until it is too late. This is particularly sad when it is very treatable if caught early on.

Colon Cancer Concern (CCC) is the UK's leading national charity dedicated to reducing deaths from bowel cancer. With your support, CCC can reach out to many more people and help save the lives of thousands who are at risk of developing bowel cancer in their lifetimes. Please make a donation to CCC today.

How the CCC helped me...

I know that when I was diagnosed with bowel cancer, I didn't know where to turn. Fortunately, I contacted CCC and their advice and support helped me to make some tough decisions at a time when I felt vulnerable and alone.

As CCC helped me, so they want to help others, but as a voluntary organisation, they can't do it without your assistance.

Judy Place, Birmingham

Call our Infoline now on:
08708 506050
or visit www.coloncancer.org.uk for discreet advice, support and information

Colon Cancer Concern, 9 Rickett Street, London SW6 1RU   Registered Charity No 1071038

Send your cheque (made payable to Colon Cancer Concern) to Colon Cancer Concern, 9 Ricket Street, London SW6 1RU or call Karen on **020 7381 9711.**

Name: _____   Ref RD

Address: _____

Postcode: _____   *thanks for*
                                                         your support!
Telephone: _____   Email: _____

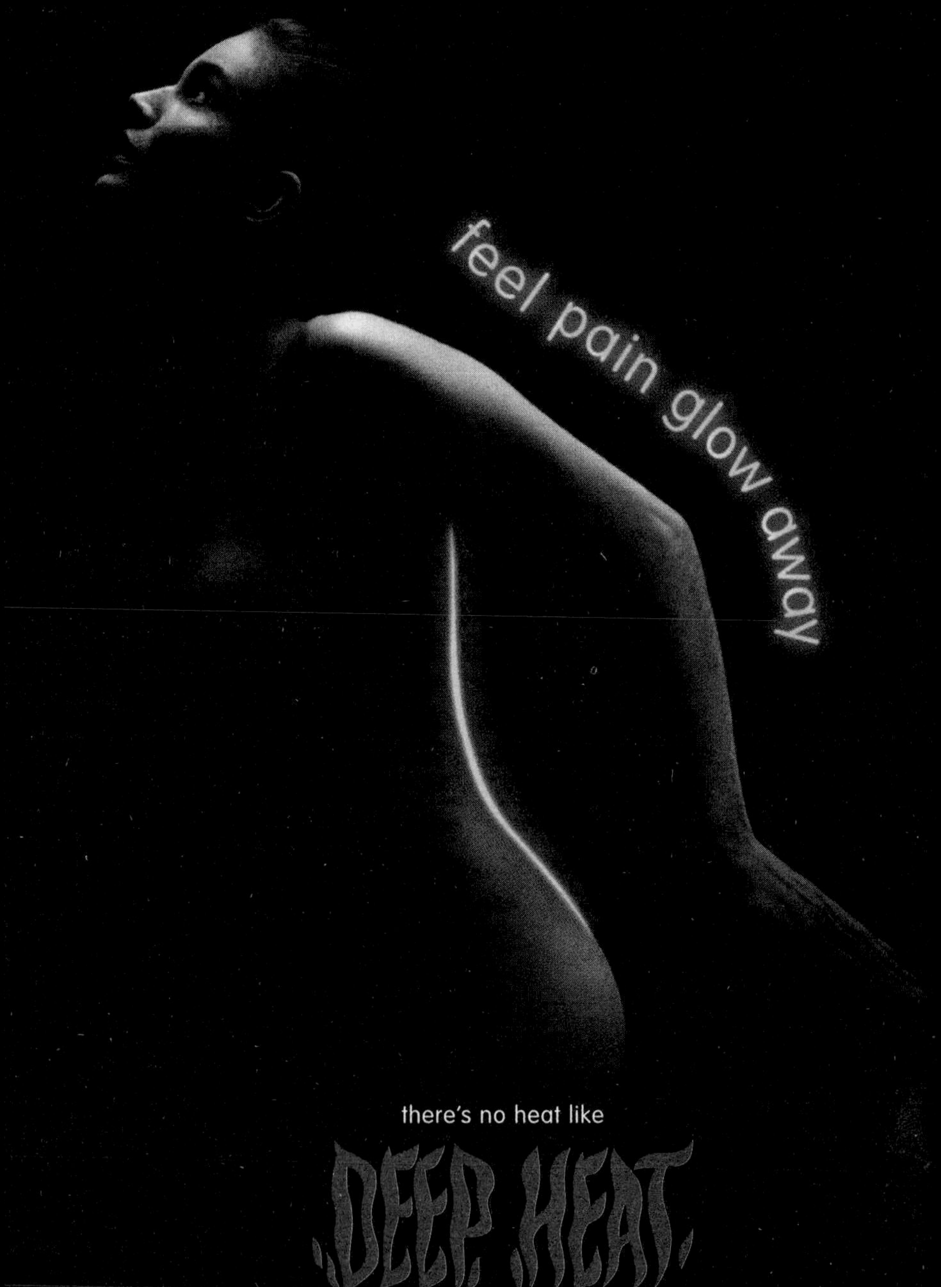

feel pain glow away

there's no heat like

DEEP HEAT

Deep Heat is available as Spray or Rub for the relief of muscular aches and pains. Always read the labe

The Eat-Less Hormone

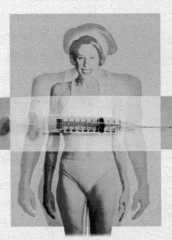

STEVE BLOOM, Professor of Endocrinology at Imperial College, London, wanted to know what mechanism in the body made people feel less hungry after a meal. "It seems to be due to a hormone called PYY," he says. Then he discovered that overweight people appear to produce less PYY than people who are thinner.

So Bloom did the obvious: he and colleagues injected obese people with PYY and then fed them a buffet lunch, carefully tracking how much food everyone ate.

The subjects downed about 400 calories less than when they were given a placebo. Even better, the effects seemed to linger. People also ate less in the 12 hours after receiving the hormone.

Now Bloom is working on another study, giving overweight people daily injections. If they lose weight, PYY may one day be available as a prescription.

A WRISTBAND NAUSEA CURE?

ACUPRESSURE WRISTBANDS really can quell nausea—if you expect them to. Researchers at the University of Rochester Cancer Centre in New York State recently completed the largest study to date of the bands, which are believed to suppress nausea by stimulating acupressure points.

Psychologist Joseph Roscoe and colleagues tested them on 700 patients who had nausea from chemotherapy. On average, those who wore the Sea-Band (a typical acupressure wristband, about £8 for a pair) and believed it would help, reported 28 per cent less nausea on the day of treatment than those who didn't wear any wristband. They also used less anti-nausea medication. Consult your doctor before you try it.

PHOTO-ILLUSTRATIONS BY MARGARET RIEGEL

Rendezvous in Lima

Nick Lopez's shanty-town dignity gave my life a new perspective

BY ELAINE PAIGE

IT WAS CHRISTMAS 2001, and I was in *The King & I* at the London Palladium. My career has always been at the centre of my life. I was a workaholic, but having just lost my adored mother, I did as she'd asked before she died: I took a year's sabbatical. I also made another decision. I'd fly to Peru to meet a young man called Nick Lopez.

Ten years earlier, a friend told me about the charity EveryChild. By giving £15 a month, you could help a youth and their family in a developing country. Something about this appealed. Here was a way I could have some sort of relationship with an individual child.

Which is how Nick came into my life. He was five, living with his parents Dilia, a nurse, and Carlos, a building worker, and, later, his two younger brothers in a shanty town above Lima.

A long way from the West End: Elaine Paige with Nick in Lima, Peru

My monthly donation would be administered by the charity's offices in Lima and via them Nick and I could write to each other about our lives and exchange photographs.

In time, it became clear that Nick and his family had to struggle to get by. I had no way of telling whether my stories of appearing in West End

33

musicals would make any sense at all.

But I felt from his letters and drawings that he enjoyed this contact with a completely alien world. I certainly enjoyed reading about his life and ambitions. As he grew older, he wrote about the hens

'I was nervous. I sensed a well of emotion that I wanted to keep in check'

and ducklings he was raising in their yard and how his dearest wish was to become a vet.

When he was eight he sent me my favourite photograph, which I keep to this day on the desk in my office. Dark-haired with a nice open face, suddenly Nick was growing up fast.

And here I was on my way to Lima at last to meet him in person. I don't know exactly what I was expecting to find, but knowing our lives were so different, would we have anything to say to each other? Preparing to meet Nick for the first time was a little like a first night. I was nervous. I could sense a well of emotion that I wanted to keep in check. If I broke down, I felt he'd be embarrassed.

It turned out to be an experience that I'll never forget. The poverty shocked me. Nick and his family live in a two-roomed house with a corrugated roof, earth on the floor and scavenged furniture.

Nick turned out to be a sweet, gentle, rather shy 15-year-old with beautiful manners and real dignity. He was keen to show me his small "farmyard" behind the house where, even in rain-starved Lima, he'd made a pond for his chicks and ducklings, which he sells for £1.50 each.

I'd thought long and hard about what gifts to bring him. I'd been told that lavish presents would single him out in that close-knit community and, anyway, I wanted to give him and his family something practical. So I bought sweatshirts for each of them; pens, pencils and notebooks for the three boys; and, for Nick, two books in Spanish about raising hens. When he saw them his face broke into a grin and suddenly he was shy no more.

I was coping fine through all this. But then his mother started thanking me in Spanish and, as her eyes filled with tears, mine did too.

I'm determined now to keep in touch with Nick even when he's 18 and outgrows the sponsorship scheme. Meeting him has set my life in a new perspective. It's made me re-evaluate my priorities.

As told to RICHARD BARBER

For more about EveryChild, go to www.everychild.org.uk or call 0845 660 8000.

To be a professional comic, all you need is a jacket and a bad childhood.

JEFFREY ROSS, US comedian

Travel-lines

We have got some fabulous ideas on where to take your next holiday. Whether it be a wonderful break in the UK or holiday overseas. For further information please tick the Reader Reply box.

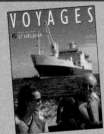

Dare to be different

Come aboard the Royal Mail Ship St Helena and sail to the stunning, remote and unspoiled South Atlantic islands of St Helena, Ascension or Tristan da Cunha.

Short fly/cruise/stay options from 10 days upwards, all year round, flying via Ascension Island or Cape Town. Longer options (up to 31 days) for blue water voyages between UK and South Africa. For brochure call 0207 816 4800/1 quoting ref. RD04 or visit www.rms-st-helena.com.

With over 65 destinations world wide, Bridge offers a city break to suit every taste and budget. From modest family-run properties to luxury hotels, and transport options including Eurostar and more flights from your local airport than ever

before, the only difficulty will be deciding where to go first! For a copy of your brochure or to book call 0870 191 4052 quoting EC04RD or click www.bridge-travel.co.uk.
ABTA: V5361, ATOL: 3334.

Come and explore

The 43rd National Boat Caravan and Outdoor Show (NEC, Birmingham, 14–22 February 2004) will host the UK's largest display of caravans, motorhomes, boats, camping equipment and outdoor leisurewear. 0870 730 0963. www.boatandcaravan.com
The home of the great outdoors

We've stayed with you for 300 years. Isn't it time you spent a few days with us? 2004 sees the 300th anniversary of British Gibraltar. And as we are proud of being British we'll be celebrating the event in grand style. Our year-long festivities will offer something for everyone. With Military parades and spectacles, unique exhibitions andspecially staged sporting events.

Take away the worry not the adventure on a Journeys of Distinction fully escorted tour to New Zealand. Journeys of Distinction feature 27 day leisurely itineraries with a minimum of two nights at every point. Celebrating over 30 years in travel, request a brochure today to discover why so many Journeys of Distinction guests return year after year. Journeys of Distinction - Often Copied, Never Equalled. www.jod.uk.com or tel: 01704 883000

Share good times with nice people.
If you like spending time with new friends, you'll enjoy a
Wallace Arnold Holiday. Choose a fully escorted holiday
from beautiful and varied destinations throughout Britain
and Ireland.
You'll enjoy an unrivalled level of customer service along
with the convenience of local joining points, our Total
Luggage Handling Service and luxury coach travel.
To order your brochure call 0845 756 6665 quoting
RDP040.

**Journey to the Centre of the
Earth with Smyril Line!**

Jules Verne set his classic
adventure novel around the
North Atlantic islands, capturing
the mystery of the **Faroe Islands**
and **Iceland** – the legendary
doorway to the centre of the earth. Smyril Line
will take you on a journey of a lifetime to these -
and other breathtaking destinations, sailing on its
highly acclaimed new luxury cruise ferry Norrona.
For a free colour brochure, call 0870 850 5678
(ref RD) or visit www.smyril-line.com

ALL IN A DAY'S WORK

Among the attractions when I worked at the Blackpool Tower was a lady who read palms, told fortunes and predicted the future.

On a very cold, windy winter afternoon, I met this clairvoyant on the staircase and asked how business had been that day.

She replied that she had only had two customers and added, "If I'd known things were going to be that quiet I wouldn't have bothered to open."

IAIN MACPHERSON, Thornton, Lancashire

When a woman requested a whole roast chicken from the butcher I work with, he didn't let on that the bird he presented her was the last one in the shop.

"Do you have one that's a little larger?" she asked.

"Of course," said the butcher. He took the chicken behind the counter, away from view, and made a lot of noise, as if he was searching for just the right chicken. He then showed the same bird to her.

"That's better," she said. "But do you have one with a little more meat on it?"

He took the chicken, repeated the charade and offered it to the customer a third time.

"That's great," said the woman. "I'll take all three."

MELANIE BECK

Operating high-pressure boilers can be stressful—like the time my two colleagues and I discovered a potentially dangerous leak in a boiler. Scorching steam was billowing out, filling up the room and decreasing visibility.

"I hope this doesn't get any

'I have an idea: let's start thinking outside the box'

SEAN HARRINGTON

customers. Here are a few choice ones, as reported in the business press:

• Compaq changed the command "Press Any Key" to "Press Return Key" because of the flood of calls asking where the "Any" key was.

• An AST Computer customer was asked to send copies of her defective diskettes. A few days later a letter arrived from the caller along with photocopies of the floppies.

• A Dell customer called to say he couldn't get his computer to fax. The technician discovered the man was trying to fax a paper by holding it in front of his monitor.

bigger," said one colleague. "I don't want this steam to be the last thing I see in this world."

"That wouldn't be so bad," my other colleague replied. "So long as it's not the first thing you see in the next." ROGER WILDEMAN

D URING AN inspection at a factory, I noticed a large red book on a table. It was extremely tatty—covered in stains from spilt drinks, cigarette burns, and had damaged edges from being dropped on the floor.

When I asked an employee about the purpose of this volume, I was informed that it was the company "accident book".

IAN LUBBOCK, Bexhill, East Sussex

C USTOMER SERVICE desks at computer companies are constantly bombarded with phone calls from some very confused

M Y FATHER'S pager beeped, summoning him to the hospital where he is an anaesthetist.

As he raced towards the hospital, a police car sped up behind him— lights flashing, siren blaring.

He had no time to stop, so Dad hung his stethoscope out the window to signal that he was on an emergency call.

Within seconds came the police officer's response: a pair of handcuffs flapping outside the police-car window. NICHOLAS BANKS

£ You could earn £100 for your story.
See "It's a Funny Old World" on page 13

DON'T FORGET THE

in the Kitchen

Healthy Eating

Making simple changes to your diet such as eating less fat and salt can greatly improve your overall well-being. This month our recipes and tips aim to show you just how easy this can be.

FISH STOCK

Most people eat more salt than they need and much of that comes from the processed foods in our everyday diet, such as simple things like stock cubes. So, try this recipe for fish stock – it's salt-free, simple to prepare and can transform all kinds of fish dishes.

Makes about 1.2 litres

900g trimmings from white fish, including skin, bones and heads without gills or 400g of inexpensive white fish such as pollock
1 onion, thinly sliced
4 sprigs parsley
2 bay leaves
2 carrots, thinly sliced
2 celery sticks, thinly sliced
4 black peppercorns
1.3 litres boiling water

Rinse the fish well, then place in a large saucepan. Add all the other ingredients, bring back to the boil then reduce the heat and simmer gently for 30 minutes, skimming off the froth as it appears on the surface. Remove from the heat and leave to cool for 10 minutes, then strain the stock through a fine sieve into a heatproof bowl. Discard the fish trimmings and vegetables. Use at once or cool and chill. It will keep in the refridgerator for up to two days, or can be frozen for up to one month.

SIMPLE SEAFOOD BROTH

Serves 4

1 litre fish stock
1/4 tsp saffron threads
85g mussels, cooked and shelled
85g shelled scallops cut into thin slices
85g peeled and deveined raw king prawns
85g plaice fillet, skinned and cut into strips
2 tomatoes, skinned and diced
1 courgette, finely diced
snipped fresh chives

Add the mussels, prawns, scallops and strips of plaice to simmering fish stock. Stir, then heat until simmering gently again. Add the tomatoes and courgettes then season to taste. Simmer the soup for 3 minutes. Ladle the soup into warm bowls and scatter chives over to garnish. Serve at once with warm French bread.

Recipes and Photos from Reader's Digest Soups and Casseroles in the Eat Well Live Well series RRP £18.99

Unfortunately, over 90% of us are not getting the **full benefit of whole grain** everyday[†].

In fact, health experts recommend eating **3 servings of whole grain a day.**

([†]according to a recent survey in Great Britain)

Whole Grain
Help your heart with a healthy start!*

People with a healthy heart tend to eat more whole grain foods as part of a healthy lifestyle.

Today's busy lifestyles make it hard to find the time to eat healthily. There are some easy ways to start and one of them is whole grain.

WHOLE GRAIN

www.wholegrain.co.uk

as part of a low fat diet and healthy lifestyle

Nestlé Bitesize Shredded Wheat

Nestlé Fruitful Shredded Wheat

Nestlé Honey Nut Shredded Wheat

Nestlé Shredded Wheat 100% WHOLE GRAIN WHEAT

LOW-FAT CAKE!

Try this simple low-fat recipe to satisfy your taste for sweet foods while cutting down on fat.
Serves 4

3 eggs
40g caster sugar
70g sieved flour
1 tbsp skimmed milk
1tsp grated lemon rind

Whisk the eggs and sugar together until thick. Fold in flour and then add the milk and lemon rind. Spoon into an 18 cm cake tin and bake at 180°C (350°F, Gas 4) for 20 minutes until risen. Allow to cool. Slice in half, fill with low-fat yogurt and fruit. Spread more yogurt and fruit on top and serve.

Recipe and Photo from Reader's Digest Eating for Good Health in the Health and Healing the Natural Way Series RRP £18.99

MARINATED SALMON

This tasty salmon recipe is a perfect choice to help you keep your overall cholesterol levels low, as salmon, pulses, fruits and vegetables actually lower 'bad' cholesterol and reduce the blood's ability to clot and clog up the arteries.
Serves 4

4 salmon steaks (175g each)
zest and juice of 1 orange
2 tbsp vegetable oil
3 thin slices of fresh ginger, shredded
1/2 tsp coriander seeds
3 cloves
salt and black pepper

Mix together all the marinade ingredients in a large, shallow, glass or ceramic dish. Add the fish and turn to coat. Cover and chill for 2 hours, turning the steaks after about 1 hour. When ready to cook, heat a griddle or heavy-based frying pan over a high heat until very hot. Brush with a little oil. Lift the fish out of the marinade and remove any flavourings stuck to the flesh. Place the fish on the hot griddle or pan and immediately reduce the heat to medium-low. Cook for 3 to 5 minutes or until the fish lifts easily away, turn and cook for a further 3 minutes, or until cooked through, and serve at once with wild rice and mangetout peas.

Recipe and Photo from Reader's Digest Great British Dishes The Healthy Way RRP £24.99

The smallest deed is greater than the grandest intention

PATTI LABELLE, singer

All music is connected, especially in a little place like England. Nothing comes from nothing at all

MICK JAGGER

It's hard to make New Year's resolutions when you're already perfectly behaved.

JUDITH MARTIN, "Miss Manners", etiquette expert

If you tell the truth, you don't need a long memory

JESSE VENTURA, politician and TV presenter

I've seen "karma" slap people in the face. You have to be good to people. It really does come around.

KIRSTEN DUNST, actress

Don't judge a book by its cover until you've read the book

quoted by JAMIE LEE CURTIS, actress

The key to success? Work hard, stay focused and marry a Kennedy.

ARNOLD SCHWARZENNEGER, actor and governor of California

My mother always used to say, "The older you get, the better you get. Unless you're a banana."

BETTY WHITE, actress

Who said it?

Raising kids makes most people, including me, grow up at least a little

a) Cher
b) Madonna
c) Paul McCartney

FOR ANSWER, SEE BELOW

b) Madonna

43

Marathon OF Miracles

Michael Watson challenged only himself, but won this nation's heart | BY DAVID MOLLER

ON A SPRING EVENING, Lennard Ballack was crossing a road in Islington, north London. The lights were red for traffic—yet one car edged forward, ignoring pedestrians. Ballack signalled the car to wait. As he continued to the housing estate where he lived, the same car pulled up and three men got out. They advanced on him menacingly.

Len Ballack knew he was in big trouble, but as his opponents closed in, a massively muscled man walked up and asked, "Any problems, Len?" The men froze. "My God!" said one. "It's Michael Watson." They turned and fled.

"Thanks, Mike," said Len Ballack, his heart still pounding. Len knew that Michael Watson was just two weeks away from a match with Nigel Benn, a middleweight with a record of 22 fights and 22 knockouts. The 24-year old

STEFAN ROUSSEAU/PA PHOTOS

Legendary boxer
Michael Watson (right)
with Lennard Ballack,
the friend who stood by
him for 12 long years

boxer could have been stabbed, damaged his fists or risked sanctions from the British Boxing Board of Control for getting involved in a street brawl.

Two weeks later Watson beat Benn and, like other neighbours and friends in Hackney, Lennard Ballack was thrilled. Michael Watson's career now took off. He became Commonwealth champion, then faced Chris Eubank for the world super middleweight title.

Already leading on points, Michael felled Eubank in the eleventh round. But Eubank suddenly surged back and Michael went down to a vicious uppercut. He stood up, groggy, but minutes later collapsed in his corner.

For seven minutes Michael lay unconscious, before a "ringside" doctor finally got to him—and then he had neither the equipment nor expertise to resuscitate the boxer. It was 28 minutes before he reached hospital where doctors suspected bleeding in his brain. When neurosurgeon Peter Hamlyn opened Michael's skull two hours later, he found a blood clot the size of a saucer. Later, Hamlyn would have to operate five more times to relieve the pressure in Watson's skull. In his notes, the surgeon predicted, "Watson will never run again, never move his left side, walk or speak smoothly." *

Lennard Ballack was devastated. When he visited his former rescuer,

---

* Watson won a suit against the British Boxing Board of Control over lack of medical care at the Eubank fight. The Board appealed, lost and then put itself into administration, unable to pay the £1.4 million award made against it. Medical arrangements have now improved.

he was lying motionless in intensive care, surrounded by tubes and wires.

MICHAEL lay comatose, on the brink of death, for 40 long days. Even after that, all he could do on his own was breathe. When the boxer was moved to a rehabilitation hospital, Lennard found it no less devastating to visit him. "Michael?" he called, gently. It took Michael about two minutes to focus his eyes and register his friend, and another two for him to raise his right hand. Lennard sat there holding it, his own hand dwarfed by the massive paw.

EIGHT MONTHS LATER, after intensive physical and mental therapy, Michael was finally able to go home to his mother Joan Watson's care. Though at first Michael needed other carers and physios, Lennard later began helping out. For him the decision was simple: Michael had stood by him in trouble. It was his turn to do the same. He quit his well-paid job with a building firm to be at Michael's side, encouraging, humouring and cajoling him.

AS MONTHS became years, Michael's speech improved, although it was still slow and slurred. Eventually he learned to walk leaning on Lennard's left shoulder, leaving space for his left leg to swing outwards, then manoeuvring himself forwards on his good right leg.

In autumn 2002, Lennard took the former boxer to Peter Hamlyn for a check-up. Hamlyn mentioned that he

Chris Eubank catches Watson off-guard during the match that will leave the British fighter with brain injuries

---

captained a team that raised funds during the London Marathon for the Brain and Spine Foundation, a charity that Hamlyn himself had started.

"Have you ever actually run the marathon yourself?" Michael asked.

"Well, no, I haven't."

"Don't you think you should?"

Hamlyn paused, taken aback.

"If you do it, I will too," said Michael. Hamlyn agreed. The great adventure had begun.

SIX MONTHS LATER, the sun is glittering on the Thames off Greenwich as 32,746 runners surge forward for the start of the 2003 London Marathon. At the rear of the field, with the rest of Hamlyn's group, Michael Watson takes the first steps of his marathon, closely watched by Lennard Ballack. Thrusting out with his good right side, he pivots carefully with his left leg, as if dragging a ball and chain.

Within half an hour they are miles behind the rest of the field, but crowds, alerted to Michael by the media, linger to see him pass. Hamlyn and a dozen others in yellow T-shirts jangle buckets to collect money.

"Hey look! They've saved the best till last," shouts one woman. For many, it is the first time they have seen, or even heard of, the legendary boxer in

12 years. A girl asks for a kiss. Michael proffers a cheek. "One is free. But if you want another, I'll have to charge."

Bus drivers halt their vehicles so the fund-raisers can have a quick whip-round among passengers. A lone, very, very late marathon starter overtakes them.

"Shall we chase him?" asks Hamlyn.

"Nah," Michael responds. "I'm not warmed up yet."

By late morning the main marathon

By evening of the first day Michael is still on the Woolwich Road—just five miles from the start.

IT'S DAY TWO AND MICHAEL, having slept overnight in a hotel, sets off again from the exact spot he left the day before. The marathon's main event is long over, but clusters of people have gathered to cheer him on.

Michael and Lennard are joined for a while by 14-year-old Alex Robinson

WATSON WILL NEVER
run again, move his left side, walk or speak smoothly

is over and Paula Radcliffe has set a new women's world record. Michael has covered just two and a half of the 26 miles. The plan has always been that he will not walk further than this at a stretch, so great are the demands he is making of his body. He boards the double-decker support bus following him for a meal and a two-hour sleep.

It's early afternoon when he hits the road again for another two-and-a-half mile stint, and on Woolwich High Street, Wayne Robinson, landlord of the Mitre pub, has already collected some £160 from customers. About 100 have stayed on until Michael appears.

"It's great of you people to make such an effort," Watson tells them over the pub's loudspeaker. "I really appreciate that." Later, Robinson delivers more contributions bringing the pub's total to more than £220.

from Norfolk, who arrives in a wheelchair pushed by his father. Knocked over by a car, he has the same partial paralysis as Michael and the same hesitant, mumbled speech. Until today he has walked little more than the width of a room unaided. For a while, dragging his left leg, Alex is just able to keep up. But by the time they reach the famous tea clipper Cutty Sark, the boy's feet are blistered and extremely painful. Patrick Drayton, a trainer for world heavyweight champion Lennox Lewis, who is helping Michael and the team, sits Alex down on the pavement, massages his feet and puts on plasters.

"You're not going to be sitting round here all morning are you, Alex?" Michael teases. Alex grins and mumbles, "I'll soon catch you up." Refusing a wheelchair, Alex ploughs on for another half mile.

Alex's determination resonates deeply with Michael. It reminds him of a boxing fund-raiser held for him at Legends nightclub in Barking in 1998. Len had started to get the wheelchair out of the back, but Michael had already heaved himself out of the car. "I won't need the chair tonight," he told Len. He looked at the 20 yards to the entrance. *I can do this*, he told himself.

"Just take your time, Michael," Lennard murmured. "There's no way they're going to start the evening without you."

Slowly, agonisingly, the boxer shuffled forward, pausing every few steps to regain his balance. As he entered the club, some of the most hard-bitten figures in the boxing world were dumbstruck, hefty arms hanging loosely by their sides. These men knew how desperately injured Michael had been. To some it seemed a miracle and tears pricked the eyes of gnarled and battered faces.

DAY THREE AND MICHAEL is heading for Tower Bridge. A steady procession of celebs—boxers, footballers, actors—joins him, waving buckets at passers-by and motorists halted in traffic.

The bridge itself is a tough place for Michael to be. It was here that pre-match photos of him and Nigel Benn were taken in 1989—when everything seemed possible for Michael, even the world championship.

But despite the memories, Michael has his usual serene smile as he moves off the bridge. Lennard Ballack has never known the former boxer to show

bitterness. Michael refers to his 1991 fight with Eubank as the "accident" and says that, in an odd way, it was his salvation. "This was the only way that God could get hold of me." He firmly believes it is now his destiny to raise people's spirits, to show what can be done to overcome appalling injuries.

BY THE FOURTH DAY, Michael's tremendous slog has taken hold of the city's imagination. As he lopes between the high-rise buildings of Canary Wharf, it's like a New York ticker-tape parade. Hundreds crowd against the windows and throng pavements to catch a glimpse of him.

During a lunch stop, Lennard checks Michael's left foot. Already rubbed raw, it's getting worse. The problem has been plaguing Michael ever since he went to a boxer's training camp a month ago to get himself in shape for the marathon. At first, it had taken Michael nearly an hour to drag himself round the 1.1-mile stone track at the camp in Cornwall. But in time, with help from trainers and physiotherapists, Michael was eventually able to let go of Lennard's shoulder and do a full circuit on his own. But there was still a problem with the way his left heel was hitting the ground.

A pair of training shoes, with internal supports, has helped minimise damage to the Achilles tendon, but despite massage and other treatments the problem of recurring blisters remained.

As they resume the walk after lunch,

Johnny Green/PA Photos

Watson reaches the finishing line of the London Marathon. With him is Chris Eubank

Lennard begins to wonder if Michael can—or even should—make it through another two days to the finish line. He says, "If you feel that you can't do it, Mike, there'll be no shame about that."

IT'S DAY FIVE and Michael mania is spreading. People travel in from outside London to cheer him on. Sporting figures take turns walking with him: among them heavyweight boxer Audley Harrison, promoter Frank Warren, and Charlton footballer Jason Euell.

Money pours in—drivers of the most beat-up vehicles hand over £50 or more; a tramp emerges from a pile of cardboard to donate a precious 70p.

Michael is finding it difficult to stay focused, with so many wanting to shake his hand, wish him luck and thank him for his inspiration. Suddenly,

his foot clips a brick tree-surround and he pitches forward. Lennard—ever alert—dives in front of Michael's falling body, arching his back to take the former boxer's weight. It works: the two scramble to their feet almost unscathed. Michael puts a hand on Lennard's shoulder and murmurs, "Thanks, mate. That's why I have got you beside me in my life."

SATURDAY, APRIL 19, the last day of Michael's tremendous tramp. His old opponent Chris Eubank has joined Michael for the final mile. As the two men head towards Parliament Square, a thousand-strong crowd breaks into

IT'S THE SLOWEST TIME
in the marathon's history—six days, two hours, 27 minutes

raucous song: "We're Walking in a Watson Wonderland". "Is that for me?" Michael asks. "I think it could be, Mike," says Lennard.

In The Mall, as Michael approaches the London Marathon finishing line (re-erected in his honour), helpers, carers, fund-raisers and well-wishers—even Lennard Ballack—step back, leaving Michael to complete the final yards on his own.

At last Michael Watson crosses the line, punching the air as an ecstatic roar erupts from the crowd. It's the slowest time in the marathon's history—six days, two hours, 27 minutes and 17 seconds.

Later, when celebrations were over and the two men were alone again, Lennard said, "I told you that you were going to deal with this—and in a fine style." Michael replied, "I couldn't have done it without you, Len, standing alongside of me."

In all, Michael Watson raised some £250,000 for charity. More than that, he gave his nation an inspiring display of the resilience of the human spirit.

Last October, Michael Watson was presented with a special award for services to boxing—for completing the London Marathon—by the British Boxing Board of Control.

If you would like to donate to the Brain and Spine Foundation, telephone 020 7793 5900 or go to www.brainandspine.org.uk.

MORAL FIBRES

At a dance, I was with a group of friends who were discussing the designer names of their ties.

As I wasn't wearing my glasses, I asked a woman sitting nearby to check mine for me.

My friends roared with laughter when she took a look and answered, "Polly Ester".

STAN FROST, Llandudno, Conwy

THE LUCK OF THE IRISH

Sign spotted in Dublin: "Fine To Park Here".

JUNE NEWMAN, Selsey, West Sussex

Our Tax Hell

Revealed: What Britons want to pay
What they think they pay
And what they really do pay

BY DAVID MOLLER

THERE YOU ARE, sitting staring at your tax return, thinking, *why does it have to be so complicated?* A cynic might say one reason is to confuse us about how much we actually pay. That way, the wisdom goes, we won't resent our taxes.

Well, we've got news for the politicians. We *are* confused. And we *do* resent our taxes.

Reader's Digest commissioned MORI to conduct

ILLUSTRATED BY PAQUEBOT

an exclusive poll for the purpose of learning, for the first time, what Britons really think about tax fairness. Our key findings:

• The maximum tax burden that Britons on average feel a family of four should bear is 26 per cent of its total income. (In fact, most Britons pay far more than this.) That's 26 per cent for *all* direct and indirect taxes combined: income tax, National Insurance payments, council tax, road tax, petrol excise duty, VAT and all other forms of indirect taxes.

• Another crucial finding is Britons' personal unhappiness with the amount that they themselves pay in taxes. More than two thirds—68 per cent—of all working people say that their total tax payments are "too high".

• The reality is worse than people imagine. Respondents across all income groups wildly *underestimate* their own and other families' overall tax burdens. For example, the average Briton thinks a family earning £25,000 pays only 21 per cent of its income in taxes when the figure is really 38 per cent.

This broad dissatisfaction with taxes has not always been the case. A poll during 1997's general election showed that 63 per cent of the public didn't believe Labour's promise not to raise taxes—yet voters went on to elect a Labour government by a landslide.

"There must have been tacit agreement that the public would accept some increase in taxes in return for better public services," says Professor Robert Worcester, chairman of MORI, a pollster with 35 years' experience and specialist adviser to the House of Commons Treasury Select Committee. After reviewing our poll findings he reports: "Things have changed big time."

Respondents we contacted after completing the poll expressed profound dissatisfaction with the status

What We *Want* to Pay

Amount of tax the average Briton considers fair

INCOME £25,000

14%

What we *really* pay 38%

INCOME £50,000

20%

What we *really* pay 40%

INCOME £100,000

26%

What we *really* pay 43%

quo. "I think taxes have reached a point where they possibly discourage people from contributing to the economy," argues Joanna Kidd, a 33-year-old self-employed hairdresser and mother of three who lives in Cramlington, Northumberland.

"When my husband, a painter and decorator, is offered overtime, he often wonders whether it is worth doing if so much is taken away before it gets into his pocket. There must be thousands like him."

Says Neil Hemming, a 40-year-old car assembly worker living in Birmingham, "Even when you get the occasional pay rise, so much of it is clawed back in rising council tax, petrol tax and all the other taxes so cleverly hidden away in the woodwork."

Surprisingly, our poll produced little evidence that those on lower incomes feel that the rich should be squeezed until the pips squeak.

On the contrary, the Reader's Digest poll found evidence that Britons think we are *all* overtaxed.

The poll was administered by phone to a cross section of 1,003 Britons. For each question, we asked respondents to think about "not just income tax but National Insurance payments, VAT,

Britons agree no **family** should pay more than **26%** tax

council tax and any other form of taxes you or anyone in your household pays."

First, we questioned Britons about tax fairness. "What", we asked, "would be a *fair* amount for a family to pay in total taxes if their total household income is £100,000 a year?"

Then we asked the respondents to consider the same question for various families of four, each of which earned a different income. Throughout, we evaluated average responses.

Despite the often-heard belief that the poor and middle class resent "the privileged", Britons earning less than £15,000 themselves agree that 23 per cent is a fair tax burden for a family of four earning £100,000 a year. Those in the middle-income range suggest 27 per cent, and top earners feel 32 per cent would be justified. The average response overall from those polled is that the family should pay no more than 26 per cent in total taxes.

We also asked, "About what percentage of your total income do you think you pay every year, when you add all these taxes together?" Then we asked respondents to consider the same question for the various families

What We *Think* We Pay

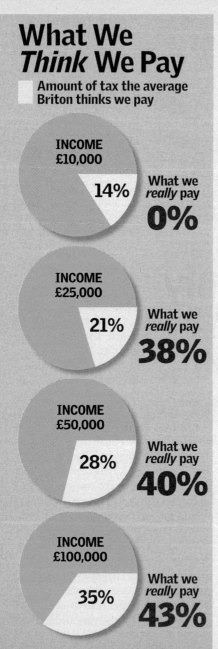

Amount of tax the average Briton thinks we pay

INCOME £10,000

14%

What we *really* pay

0%

INCOME £25,000

21%

What we *really* pay

38%

INCOME £50,000

28%

What we *really* pay

40%

INCOME £100,000

35%

What we *really* pay

43%

of four. We found that respondents did a poor job estimating their own overall taxes and the taxes paid by other families.

To find out what people *actually* pay, we'd commissioned a special survey from leading business and financial advisers Grant Thornton. Taking a hypothetical family living in Andover, Hampshire, with children aged 11 and 13, where the husband earns 75 per cent of the income and his wife 25 per cent, Grant Thornton figures suggest that on an income of £25,000 a year the family will see their total tax bite soar to an estimated 38 per cent. This is almost double the 21 per cent burden estimated by our respondents.

It gets worse. A family on £50,000 will see 40 per cent of their hard-earned cash slither away into the pockets of the state—not the average of 28 per cent guessed at in our poll.

Those on £100,000? Oops! 43 per cent—not the 35 per cent optimistically estimated by our respondents.

The only good news is for the £10,000-a-year family which, thanks to tax credits, ends up losing none of its income in taxes, rather than the 14 per cent estimated by those we polled.

Asked to estimate their *own* overall tax burden, respondents don't do much better. The mean response of 27 per cent doesn't even come close to the actual national average of 36 per cent.

Respondents we spoke to were surprised they had underestimated the taxes people pay. "I am appalled," said David Dowse, a 56-year-old self-employed designer and fitter of

The Chancellor's Tax Tricks

Don't be fooled by politicians' smoke and mirrors

GOVERNMENT and the economy are now so complicated that most of us have lost sight of the taxes we pay and the services we get back in return.

As it happens, the cost of government and public services is very high. Here's what each of us forks out every week to fund them:

Social Security: **£40.03**

Health: **£26.73**

Education: **£17.47**

Defence: **£8.15**

Interest on National Debt: **£6.50**

Public libraries: **33p**

As Gordon Brown has tried to get borrowing down and public spending up, the tax burden has in-creased. The big tax rises? National Insurance last year, tax on pension funds in Labour's first term. Then there's the extra tax the Chancellor raises by doing nothing. As the economy grows, we tend to get richer and end up paying more tax. Mr Brown has benefited from this like no other chancellor.

It's best to ignore politicians' statements on how much tax you pay. They don't tell outright untruths, but they do tell "little white lies". They may talk about direct taxes and benefits—those deemed indirect are not counted. These include company taxes, council tax, stamp duty and the taxes on spending, such as petrol.

There is one decent measure of the tax burden: the total proportion of national income taken by the Government. This includes all taxes and relates to the size of the economy. In 2002, it was about 39.6 per cent. In 1997, it was 38.9 per cent. In the international league, Britain sits in the mid-Atlantic: the US was 32.2 per cent last year; the Eurozone 46.1.

Of course, chancellors could do their best to shed light on the tax system and base their decisions on the fairest system of raising money. But they don't do that. Governments of all shades use our ignorance of tax to get us to pay the bills without complaining.

One trick is to raise money from corporations and pension funds. Most of us don't think of ourselves as paying those taxes. But the tax has to be paid by its shareholders (in smaller profits), its staff (in lower wages) or its customers (in higher prices).

Another way chancellors raise money is to let local authorities do it for them. Since 1997, council tax has gone up from 3.7 per cent of total tax to an estimated 4.6. When you think that each one per cent is four billion pounds (£1.30 a week for each of us), you can see that during the Chancellor's incumbency there's been a large shift towards making local author-ities raise more money by themselves.

The truth is there is no painless way out of paying for public services. The Chancellor would be as delighted as the rest of us if we could find one. In Norway, for example, they have one with their oil revenues. In Britain, life is more difficult.

kitchens near Lincoln. "Over the years you can see small- business people like me being slowly crushed under this dead weight of taxes."

To a remarkable extent, different groups of Britons agree they pay too much in taxes. Respondents from ethnic minorities were especially dissatisfied: a whopping 74 per cent say they pay too much.

Those working, and those with children living at home, are unhappy; 68 per cent and 67 per cent of them respectively complain about what they pay. But overall, how many of the poll's respondents say the taxes they pay are fair? Just 28 per cent.

Perhaps there is a growing appreciation that we are not getting enough back in return, in the shape of roads, schools, pensions, health services. That's the view of John Blundell, director general of the Institute of Economic Affairs. "The state only spends a small part of its billions in giving us back services," he says. "The bulk is spent nourishing the departments of state and their legions of employees." While public sector spending as a whole rose last year at a rate of 9.3 per cent, its output (delivery

60% of Britons say they are not getting value for money from their council taxes

of services to the public) increased by just 2.4 per cent.

Certainly, our poll shows a growing dissatisfaction with council tax—60 per cent judge it poor value for money. "It's a dissatisfaction that is increasing with every increase in local tax," Professor Robert Worcester confirms.

Discontent with council tax ranges from 55 per cent in Wales to 66 per cent in London. In Scotland, with a dissatisfaction level of 58 per cent, poll respondent Maureen McWatt has seen the council tax on her home outside Edinburgh rise by nearly 700 per cent over the last 25 years. "This doesn't seem to have been matched by any improvement in services," she says.

Possibly the most significant finding in our poll concerns whether respondents feel it more important to reduce taxes or keep up government spending. When asked, "Should services such as health, education and welfare be extended even if it means some increases in taxes?" just 38 per cent of respondents answered yes—compared with

MORI'S TELEPHONE OMNIBUS INTERVIEWED A NATIONALLY REPRESENTATIVE QUOTA SAMPLE OF 1,003 ADULTS AGED 16 AND OVER THROUGHOUT GREAT BRITAIN BETWEEN OCTOBER 2 AND 6, 2003

76 per cent in April 1997 and 61 per cent in November 2000, when MORI asked a similar question. Interestingly, 29 per cent think that taxes should be cut, but that people should be asked to pay a certain amount for health or education services, such as a visit to their GP or school books.

Respondent Sherland Morris, a Berkshire social worker, would favour higher taxes if it actually led to better services. "We hear that so many more billions are being spent on health, education and social services. But as someone working with families on the very lowest end of the income scale, I can only wonder, *Where has the money gone?* "

Professor Robert Worcester sums up the Reader's Digest poll findings like this: "Which ever way you look at these figures, they are sending a powerful message to the Chancellor of the Exchequer—there's a strong and growing feeling in this country that we are getting poor value for our taxes."

BELIEVE ME...

The most important thing to succeed in show business is sincerity. And if you can fake that, you've got it made.

GEORGE BURNS in How to Be Funny by Jon Macks (Simon & Schuster)

My mother said, "You won't amount to anything because you procrastinate." I said, "Just wait."

JUDY TENUTA

ALL SHOOK UP

On a recent visit to New York, we'd gone to see the Statue of Liberty and were waiting for the ferry to take us to Ellis Island, when I overheard a guide explaining the next part of the trip to a group from India. One man, returning from the gift shop, squeezed into the group and apologised for being late. "Do not worry," one of his fellow travellers told him. "We are now going to Elvis Island." TERI BOARDMAN BOGGESS

TEE FOR TWO

My five-year-old nephew Elix wanted to caddy for my brother's golf game.

   "You have to count my strokes," my brother told him. "How much is six, nine and eight?"

   "Five," answered Elix.

   "OK," said my brother. "Let's go." MIRIAM SLEIMAN, Carlton, Australia

PROTEIN POWER

Scrambled eggs (1 whole egg and 2 egg whites)
240ml skimmed or semi-skimmed milk
½ grapefruit
1 slice wholemeal toast

kcals 300, fat 7g (saturated 2g), cholesterol 215g,
sodium 440mg, carbohydrate 35g, fibre 4g, protein
24g, calcium 350mg

Change
One

7 Meals That Help You Shed Pounds

EXPECTING FOOD TO change your life may seem like a lot to ask of your bran muffin. But have you considered that eating the right food at the right time will increase your energy, help you manage your weight and ward off major illness? Study after study has demonstrated that people who lose as little as ten pounds reap all these rewards.

The meals that follow come courtesy of ChangeOne, the exclusive weight-loss plan from Reader's Digest. ChangeOne has helped millions of people lose weight one meal at a time, one week at a time. But this plan offers more than sage dieting advice.

Derived from the latest research, these meals deliver specific nutrients to help you fight disease and shed pounds. Not weight conscious? You can still benefit; just allow yourself more generous portions.

Protein Power

One good idea emerged from all the controversy surrounding high-protein diets: researchers have found that eating a meal with plenty of protein leaves you feeling more satisfied for longer when compared to a meal loaded with low-quality carbohydrates. Your body takes longer to digest protein, leading to a gradual increase in blood sugar. Many high-carbohydrate meals are absorbed quickly and send blood sugar on a roller coaster ride, taking your appetite with it and depleting your energy.

The high-protein breakfast (on the left) will carry you through the morning and, importantly, through your coffee break.

■ **MORE PROTEIN OPTIONS**

cottage cheese   smoked fish
yogurt

Disease-Fighting at Lunch

Many foods contain antioxidants, but fruits and vegetables may be the richest source. Behaving like chemical warriors, antioxidants neutralise molecules known as free radicals before arteries and other cells can be harmed. This protects you from heart disease, high blood pressure, cancer and diabetes, which is why antioxidant foods appear so much in ChangeOne.

Forget pills—antioxidants work best when consumed in foods. In fact, the Department of Health recommends we eat five portions of fruit and vegetables a day. It's less daunting than it sounds: a portion equals a piece of fruit, three tablespoons of cooked vegetables, a bowl of lettuce or a small glass of 100 per cent juice. The typical salad delivers two to three servings. This lunch dishes up at least four antioxidant-rich servings of vegetables.

■ MORE DISEASE-FIGHTERS

leafy greens	berries
citrus fruit	cantaloupe melon
red-grape juice	

Fat-burning at Dinner

The mineral calcium is the latest weight-loss star, and ChangeOne is one of the first weight-loss plans to capitalise on its power. Scientists stumbled on calcium's magic by accident. In a US study of blood pressure in obese African Americans, people who added one large tub of yogurt a day to their diet lost an average of 11 pounds of body fat in one year, even though they didn't eat less.

A follow-up study found that people on a high-calcium diet, the equivalent of more than three daily servings of dairy, lost more weight and fat than did people on a low-calcium diet—and again, both groups ate the same number of calories. Researchers believe calcium works by encouraging fat cells

FAT-BURNING AT DINNER
Sweet-and-Sour Tofu with Vegetables
8 tbsp brown rice
1 orange, cut into wedges

Serves 4
2 tbsp soy sauce
2 tbsp fresh lime juice
60ml hot water
2 tsp sugar
4 spring onions, thinly sliced
225g cabbage, coarsely chopped
1 courgette halved lengthways and cut
across into ½-cm-thick slices
1 red pepper, cored, seeded and diced
1 tin (450g) pineapple cubes
350g tofu, cut into 2cm squares
1 tbsp finely chopped fresh ginger
¼ tsp salt
⅛ tsp cayenne pepper

1. Combine soy sauce, lime juice, hot
water and sugar in a large saucepan.
Bring to the boil over medium-high heat.
Add spring onions, cabbage, courgette
and pepper. Reduce heat and simmer,
covered, for 4 minutes.
2. Add pineapple, tofu, ginger, salt and
cayenne pepper. Cover and simmer,
stirring occasionally, until heated through,
about 3 minutes. Serve with cooked rice
and orange wedges to garnish.

   per serving: kcals 450, fat 6g (saturated
1g), cholesterol 0mg, sodium 680mg,
carbohydrate 88g, fibre 11g, protein 17g,
calcium 275mg

MEDITERRANEAN SNACK
2 Roasted-Pepper Pinwheels

Flour tortilla (20cm wide) filled
with smoothly blended chickpeas
(55g), fat-free yogurt (1 tbsp),
sesame oil (½ tsp), lemon
zest (½ tsp) and juice
(2 tsp), water (2 tsp)
and pinch of salt;
topped with strips
from 1 grilled red pepper
and salad greens, and
left to chill in foil for
1 to 4 hours. Unwrap and
cut into 8 pieces. Serves 4.

per serving: kcals 90, fat 2g
(saturated 0g), cholesterol 0mg,
sodium 150mg, carbohydrate 17g,
fibre 3g, protein 3g, calcium 45mg

EAT MORE, LOSE WEIGHT
2 cricket ball size portions
of Storecupboard Stew

Serves 4
2 tins (800g) tinned chopped tomatoes
1 tin (400g) chickpeas or other pulses
300g frozen mixed vegetables
155g small pasta shapes
½ tsp each dried oregano and basil
500ml water (more if needed)

1. Combine ingredients in a pan. Place over medium heat and bring to the boil.
2. Simmer for 20 to 30 minutes, stirring occasionally until pasta is al dente.
3. Serve with 1 slice of garlic bread.

per serving: kcals 400, fat 7g (saturated 2g), cholesterol 5mg, sodium 700mg, carbohydrate 67g, fibre 8g, protein 20g, calcium 200mg

to stop "getting fatter". Instead, the cells burn extra fat without you having to go anywhere near a treadmill. This dinner features tofu; it's calcium-rich and helps lower blood cholesterol.

■ MORE FAT-BURNERS
milk	yogurt
cheese	tinned fish
calcium-fortified juice	

Mediterranean Snack
The traditional Mediterranean diet offers an abundance of fruits and vegetables, legumes, cheese and yogurt, fish, whole grains, wine and healthy fats from nuts, olives and olive oil. The fish and nuts provide filling, healthy protein; the produce delivers loads of antioxidants.

Researchers studying thousands of Greek adults found that those who most closely ate a Mediterranean diet were least likely to die from heart disease and cancer.

■ MORE MEDITERRANEAN OPTIONS
nuts	olives
fish	beans
bulgar wheat	

Eat More, Lose Weight
Yes, you can and no, this isn't a scam. Just pick foods rich in fibre. High-fibre foods have what's officially called low-energy density; that translates to few calories relative to weight, which means you can pile your plate high with these foods without fear of calorie overload.

Fibre also aids weight loss because it's filling. Most high-fibre foods take a lot of chewing, triggering your body's fullness sensors. Plus, you absorb the food more slowly so you feel full longer and are less susceptible to the hunger-inducing rise and fall of blood sugar.

■ MORE FIBRE OPTIONS
legumes	bran cereals
fruits, vegetables	Whole grain breads

HOT TOMATO

1 slice Hearty Meat Loaf, about 2.5cm thick (see ChangeOne book for recipe)

Egg noodles tossed with chopped parsley (tennis ball size)

Steamed baby courgettes drizzled with 1 tsp olive oil

kcals 390, fat 10g (saturated 3g), cholesterol 120mg, sodium 560mg, carbohydrate 45g, fibre 6g, protein 32g, calcium 55mg

Hot Tomato

Here's a finding any man could love: Harvard scientists discovered that eating plenty of pizza seems to lower the risk of prostate cancer. The protective ingredient is tomato sauce or, more specifically, lycopene in tomato sauce. It is most concentrated in cooked tomato products such as ketchup and tomato soup; cooking also makes it easier for the body to absorb.

Preliminary research on women suggests a diet rich in lycopene and tomato sauce may lower a woman's risk of breast and other cancers, as well as heart disease.

■ **MORE LYCOPENE**
pink grapefruit   watermelon

Get the ChangeOne weight-loss programme, plus tips, menus and quizzes by calling 0800 222233 (£19.99 plus £1.95 p&p). Also available from good book shops.

Our Reader's Digest colleagues in the US have created a personalised programme too. You'll get a meal plan, newsletter, recipes and more at ChangeOne.com. You'll join a community of thousands who are losing weight online.

Smart Food

Studies abound on the health benefits of eating fish: lower risk of stroke in men eating fish at least once a month; reduced risk of Alzheimer's among people eating fish at least once a week; and heart health from two weekly servings of fatty fish (salmon, tuna, sardines). Though there are concerns about mercury levels in fish, only a few are worrisome. Most people can safely eat a few servings a week.

■ **MORE GOOD FATTY FISH OPTIONS**
kipper   mackerel

SMART FOOD
Grilled or blackened salmon
1 grilled Portobello mushroom cap
Green salad with 1 tbsp reduced-fat or fat-free dressing
4 tbsp sautéed spinach
6 tbsp white rice

kcals 430, fat 16g (saturated 3g), cholesterol 55mg, sodium 570mg, carbohydrate 44g, fibre 6g, protein 28g, calcium 150mg

RD Face to Face with
Julia Roberts

you glow girl

BY LYNN SHERR

IT WASN'T QUITE WHAT YOU'D IMAGINE: Hollywood's most bankable film star, at home in California wearing sweaty workout clothes (she'd just finished a yoga class), knitting (a blanket for a friend's newborn) and confiding that, "It's tricky to swing dance in a girdle." We'll get back to the girdle. For now let's put it this way: that's Julia Roberts.

Fifteen years into a career that started with *Mystic Pizza* and won her an Oscar as *Erin Brockovich*, the *Pretty Woman* star is back with another mind-bending role. In *Mona Lisa Smile*, out next month, Roberts plays a free-thinking professor of art history who challenges the conservative, altar-bound young women of Wellesley College, a famously exclusive American single-sex institution, in the uptight 1950s. Hence the girdle, the only concession to tradition for her rebellious character.

Not bad for a girl who headed to New York after leaving school and joined the "grind"—her word—to pound out a living as a sales assistant. She paid her dues and today is praised for roles that help redefine how women can, or should, behave. She has her own production company, and she makes at least £13 million per picture.

Roberts's personal life is also soaring. In July 2002, she married Danny Moder, a cinematographer, whom she credits for her new sense of comfort.

RD: You've just turned 36. What's the best part about growing older for you?
Roberts: Nothing bothers me. No, everything bothers me. The best part is perspective.

RD: Do you think you've got wiser?
Roberts: I married a wise man. Is that getting wiser?

RD: A good marriage?
Roberts: Beyond. A friend of mine asked me recently about being in California: "What do you do out there?"

I said, "What do I do? I be married to Danny." Like I actively participate in being married to this man.

RD: In *Mona Lisa Smile*, you're accused of waging a war on marriage. And here you are, Miss Happily Married.
Roberts: It was one of the paradoxes of playing this character because I was a newly-wed. She's a woman who's not anti-marriage, but is deeply concerned that these girls will throw away so much simply to become housewives. It was a moment when the focus of my heart was being a housewife. And it was interesting to play this person who I'm not dissimilar to—and yet I've kind of morphed into the other side of that coin.

RD: I've read that you actually like housework. Tell me it's not true.
Roberts: Well, it is. This morning I did the laundry. I'm not anal, but I'm a good housekeeper.

RD: Are you telling me you don't have a cleaner? At any of your houses?

Role playing—(left to right) Roberts with Richard Gere in 1990's *Pretty Woman*; as crusader Erin Brockovich; mentoring Julia Stiles in *Mona Lisa Smile*

EVERETT COLLECTION

Lynn Sherr is a correspondent on the US ABC News television programme "20/20".

Roberts: No, we don't. If you mess it up, you should clean it up.

RD: You chose not to go to college yourself? Was it about money?

Roberts: Not really. I don't want to sit here in this amazing place in my life and say, "I was too poor to go to college." I've been given the chance to build on a lot of opportunities I didn't have as a kid. Look, we didn't have the money, though my mum probably could have scraped it together. I probably could have applied myself more at school. It just wasn't my path.

RD: At the time, did you feel you were missing something?

Roberts: My best friend went to university and every time I talked to her it sounded so great. And here I was, selling trainers and getting the subway every day. We both thought the other person's life was so much more exciting.

RD: What did you come away from Wellesley feeling about single-sex education?

Roberts: I think there's something to be said for the lack of distraction and that you're less inclined to worry about your outfit and hair. I know that my niece, who's 12, dresses in a way that is incomprehensible to me. She's now started going to an all-girls school where they have uniforms, and somewhere I feel relief for her.

RD: Was going back to a time so different from now part of the film's appeal?

Roberts: The girls in college today are of a generation where you could forget it wasn't always this easy. I'm 36 years old and even I have dealt with some of the push and pull of being a girl in a business that has its boys and its girls.

RD: What do you think it is that people respond to when you're on screen?

Roberts: I would do anything to avoid knowing because I'd become so aware of that thing. I do believe in the mystical coming together of me and certain films—that moment in time where you

She's got dogs, horses and geese, and as a child Roberts dreamed of one day becoming a vet. "I thought that I had a special kinship to animals, that somehow we were on the same cosmic plane"

play this character, then look back and think, *God, I don't know how I did it.*

RD: Which one are you talking about?
Roberts: *Pretty Woman* for one. The last time I saw it—about ten years ago— I thought, *I never stop moving. I just couldn't hop around like a bunny now.*

RD: How was it working in *Mona Lisa Smile* with these younger stars?
Roberts: I was ready with my speech about "You have to be on time", and nobody was late. They're gorgeous, talented; they just jump out at you. I mean, Julia Stiles is gorgeous.

RD: You've been married almost two years. Do you see children in your life?
Roberts: I would hope so, yeah. I can't

say we haven't talked about it. One of the strange things about being an actor is being asked personal questions by people you don't know. They say, "Well, they've been married two years, why haven't they had kids? It must be trouble." That kind of stuff gives me fits.

RD: You're now spending more time in California.
Roberts: It's kind of a new frontier for me. My husband's a Californian, so I've had to make my peace with a place obsessed with all that I find tedious.

RD: Which is?
Roberts: The narcissistic, egomaniacal, judgemental, mean-spirited sense of show business. And the examination of actors and movies.

RD: The gossip columnists basically.
Roberts: People creeping around trying to take a picture of you doing anything, going anywhere. People wait outside our house all the time. We step out to put the garbage in the bin and there's a person. Step out to walk the dog and there's a person. Step out to go shopping, there's a person.

RD: You've used your stardom to light up some important causes, especially Rett syndrome [a neurological disease mostly afflicting young girls], thanks to a child you met some years ago. Tell me about Abigail Brodsky.
Roberts: I was so taken by Abigail, who I met through my sister. We spent an afternoon with her in the park. But I'm not thinking, *Hmm, what is this syndrome?* It's just a day with my sister and this girl who she loves—and it was just fate the way it happened.

RD: Another love of yours is animals. You did a film on orang-utans. Do you love being with animals in the wild?
Roberts: I really do. And I did a film on wild horses in Mongolia. It was a truly remarkable experience.

RD: I hear that you have pet geese.
Roberts: Danny and I went to a live-stock-supplier and they had this trough that had geese and ducks in it, and they were so cute. Finally, these two friends of ours came walking in the house one day with Danny and two little geese.

RD: You have become a role model—particularly for young women—with this new film coming out. What's the message you would want to give?
Roberts: To have a greater sense of self—of self-confidence and self-respect. I didn't have that for a long time, but I think a lot of girls don't.

RD: What's the biggest misconception you think people have about you?
Roberts: That I'm fascinating.

RD: You don't think you are?
Roberts: I am to my husband—as well I should be. But I don't do anything extraordinary on a day-to-day basis. I try to be a good wife, a good family member, a good friend. I try to do all these tiny things that impact on my circle of the world. But there's nothing grand going on here.

MOTORWAY MAYHEM

Heard during a traffic update on local radio: "A ladder has been shed on lane three of the M25. Traffic is swerving to avoid it. Police are taking steps to remove it." BARBARA HEMSLEY, Lewes, East Sussex

---

PULLING THE WOOL OVER YOUR EYES

Cardiology—the science of chunky knitwear.

FALL

When a student skydiver tumbles out of control, one instructor won't let go | BY LYNN ROSELLINI

BOBO BONADIES NEVER FELT quite so free as when he was falling through the air high above the earth, wearing a jumpsuit with a parachute on his back. So when he pulled his Ford pick-up on to the grass near the drop zone at tiny Ellington Airport in northern Connecticut early one morning in May 2002, the day was full of promise. The runway, surrounded by cornfields and pastures, was empty, with only a few small planes parked precisely along one perimeter. It was 18 degrees C, sunny, with a light wind: perfect for skydiving.

Robert Bonadies, "Bobo" to his friends, was a legend at Connecticut Parachutists, the skydiving club where he was both president and instructor. "I am the greatest!" he would joke with his students as he went about checking their rigs. Before long they believed it. And with

PHOTOGRAPHED BY ROBERTO METTIFOGO

Bobo next to them on the jump plane, flashing his big smile, patting shoulders, even timid beginners began to think they could be great too.

That morning, Bonadies set about opening the clubhouse as usual. Laid off from his job as an electrician, Bonadies was planning to savour his one pure pleasure, skydiving. He would be instructing Cindy Hyland, a middle-aged mother who had completed two free falls with him, one a week earlier that had gone great.

Strolling across the runway—Bobo's favourite Frank Sinatra CD blaring from outdoor speakers—Cindy Hyland felt pretty good herself. A lifelong lover of the outdoors, she enjoyed camping and kayaking. Hyland, 43, found not only exhilaration in skydiving, but also a surprising sense of spiritual peace

When she reached back for the rip cord, she grasped only air. Seconds flew by

as she floated to earth in solitude and stillness under canopy. Maybe it was a way to escape the stresses of her job counselling HIV patients at a women's maximum security state prison. Once, she'd even brought a skydiving video of herself to show the inmates—"so they know there's a little adventure in life."

Today, as usual, Hyland had butterflies in her stomach—but she knew they would disappear when she stepped out of the door of the plane.

BONADIES, A SLENDER man with thick salt-and-pepper hair, was setting out gear in the equipment shed when he spotted her. "You all set?" he shouted, grinning. For the next hour, they practised "dirt diving", rehearsing the dive by stepping out of a mock-up of a Cessna 182 door, mounted on a four-foot platform.

The drill was this: At 10,000 feet, Hyland was to stabilise her position, check her altimeter and begin the first of three practice rip cord touches. Between 10,000 and 6,000 feet, she was to perform two more. After checking her altimeter again, she had to wave her arms, indicating that she was about to open, and then pull her chute at 5,500 feet.

On either side of her would be Bonadies and another experienced instructor, Jim Olko, an easy-going bear of a man. As certified Accelerated Freefall jump masters, the two men had logged 6,500 jumps between them and taught hundreds of students. Once in the air, the instructors would position themselves like training wheels on a bicycle, flying Hyland in an "arch", a belly-to-earth position, gripping her leg harness with one hand and her arm with the other.

Jumping at the same time, Brian Festi, a skydiving coach, would film the trio from a few feet away with a camera mounted on his helmet.

The Cessna was on the runway, propellers whirring, as the four piled in. At 12,000 feet, the student and the three veterans slapped hands in a pre-jump ritual. "This is going to be a good jump," said Bonadies. Then he pushed the door open.

Below them the rolling green hills of northern Connecticut lay like a fairyland, farms and pastures interspersed with white industrial estates.

Festi climbed out first and dangled by his hands from the wing strut. Then Bonadies positioned himself on the step above the landing gear, followed by Hyland and Olko.

Perched on the step, Bobo gave a thumbs-up. The wind roared in their ears. From then on, communication would be by hand signal. This was one of Hyland's favourite moments. Fear was gone. She stepped out into the emptiness, fell back and caught a glimpse of the plane above her before it disappeared from view.

WITH HIS CAMERA RUNNING, Festi watched the jump begin. Fanning out into three perfect arches, student and instructors quickly picked up speed, plummeting at 120mph. It was textbook perfect. Without a parachute, an object falling at that speed would hit the ground in roughly 68 seconds. An arm's length away, facing Hyland, Festi continued filming. At 10,000 feet, about ten seconds into free fall, Hyland checked her wrist altimeter and then

Cindy Hyland found skydiving exhilarating and peaceful

began her practice rip cord touches. She had repeatedly rehearsed reaching above her right hip for the bright orange rip cord that opens the main parachute. This time, though, when she reached back for the rip cord, she couldn't find it. Seconds flew by.

When Hyland tried again, Bonadies took hold of her wrist and guided her hand to the rip cord. On her third attempt, she missed again. Now Bobo looked over her backpack at Olko. *No*, he indicated with a shake of his head. *Don't let go.*

At 5,500 feet, 37 seconds into the fall, Hyland fumbled for the strap once more, this time to pull. But she lost her balance. In an instant, she was tumbling—bringing the trio into a funnel, one of the most dangerous situations. In a funnel, two or more skydivers fly on top of one another, reducing air pressure between them and increasing speed. Divers are pulled in by the suction, much like a race car stays close behind the leader of a race to take advantage of the slipstream.

With no air between them, the divers accelerated to 170mph in less than two seconds. Somersaulting through the air, they slammed into one another like wrestlers. In the chaos, Olko and Bonadies struggled desperately to turn Hyland back on to her

Robert Bonadies at the start of his skydiving career

belly so she could safely pull her chute.

Hyland, terrified, felt as if she was in a blender. Nothing existed but the smashing of elbows, knees and feet, and the roar of the wind.

BRIAN FESTI HAD STAYED near the trio by dropping into a vertical, seated dive. Now he watched in horror at the scene he was filming.

If a student's chute isn't open by 2,000 feet, the US Parachute Association requires instructors to release the student and deploy their own chutes. Students carry a computerised device called a CYPRES, which, while not foolproof, will fire the reserve chute at 750 feet. But today, Bonadies and Olko weren't thinking of themselves. They held fast to Hyland, plummeting past the cut-off point.

If I don't stop, I'm going to die, thought Festi, a softly spoken man who admired the exuberant Bonadies. *And I'm going to watch my friends die.* At 1,800 feet, Festi grabbed his rip cord. "Pull! Pull!" he screamed to the others. But the wind washed his words away.

JIM OLKO had been in dozens of funnels. "Oke" knew that experienced divers could regain stability by resuming the arch position. But Hyland was out of control and neither he nor Bonadies had a clear shot at opening her chute without bumping the other. If the 14-pound chute hit either of them at this speed, it could break an arm, a neck or knock them unconscious.

It will be easier for Bobo to open her chute without me in the way, he thought. Finally, he let go of Hyland and pulled his parachute at 1,100 feet. Now, just Bonadies was left, gripping Hyland face-to-face in a bear hug.

A skilled long-distance runner, Bonadies had trained jittery novices to compete in marathons to raise money for The Leukaemia & Lymphoma Society. If Bobo coached you, runners knew, he stuck with you to the end—he'd even walk back after he finished to run with you.

At last he managed to flip Hyland into an arch position. On his back below her, he could see the terror in her eyes and the open sky above. He reached around her hip and pulled the rip cord. An instant later, her CYPRES fired her reserve parachute.

With four seconds left, Bonadies saw his student float away, her main and reserve chutes open. But because he was on his back, he couldn't judge the distance to the ground. There were two seconds left when Bonadies rolled over and reached for his rip cord.

O LKO WATCHED his friend fall. *He's checking to make sure she's OK*, he thought in disbelief from his vantage several hundred feet higher. *He's making sure the two parachutes don't get tangled.*

Filming everything, Festi saw that Bonadies was giving her a final chance, but wouldn't have time to pull his own cord. Bobo had always seemed a larger-than-life figure, so full of joy and energy that he'd go on for ever.

Festi couldn't bear to watch what was about to happen. He looked away—and the camera turned too.

BOBO BONADIES DIED on impact. He slammed into a pasture near the airport. His chute was in working order, investigations by the Federal Aviation Authority and police later showed. But he hadn't had enough time to open it. He was too busy saving Cindy Hyland's life.

In a wake that lasted six hours, more than 1,000 people waited to pay their respects to Bobo in a queue that stretched out of the funeral home door and around the building. Some were runners; others were union colleagues. Skydivers arrived by the score.

Cindy Hyland was there, too, though she couldn't bear to go to the grave site and watch Bobo's 13-year-old daughter bury her father. "My family and I will never forget him, his courage, his dedication," she wrote in an online memorial book. "I will see Bobo in every blue sky."

Last year, the Carnegie Hero Fund Commission gave a posthumous award to Bonadies for saving Hyland's life. And 39 parachutists from across the country performed an aerial display in his honour—"Bobo's Big Dream". On a spring day, members of his running club competed in a race to raise funds for a school award given in his name.

But Bonadies's real legacy is in the hearts of his family, friends and students. Bobo, they feel, taught them how to embrace life, not run from it.

At the airport, near the drop zone where Bonadies used to float to earth on blue-sky days, his friends placed a simple marble plaque in his honour. "To my people," it reads. "Dream Big."

MATERIAL WHIRL

While working in Vienna playing the organ at a festival, my husband Peter was the guest of a woman who was able to converse in limited English.

On the first evening Peter complimented his host on a delicious salad she had made saying, "I love your dressing. What is it?"

She thanked him and, carefully examining her frock replied, "I think it is cotton."   HELEN ROYCROFT, Dublin

Doing your own ironing, digging the garden, chopping garlic

Is It Really Worth Your Time?

BY JANE SPENCER

SARAH KALLINEY doesn't have time to do her ironing, visit her parents or change the cat's litter tray. She eats out six nights a week and gets her food shopping delivered to her door. But the time-starved executive, who earns roughly £130 an hour, recently spent ten hours battling with her mobile phone company over late payments costing a few pounds.

Was that worth her time? It's a question economists are now tackling.

After decades of using time-value formulas to help firms maximise productivity, researchers are looking at how those concepts apply to the home. In an economy of convenience, where time can be purchased in everything from pre-washed lettuce to dog-walking services, these studies aim to answer questions many of us wrestle with daily: who can afford a cleaner? A gardener? Someone to organise our bills?

The household has a lot in common with a small firm, says Professor Jonathan Gershuny, director of the Institute of Social and Economic Research at Essex University. "Decisions must be made about what work is to be done, what goods must be bought. The word economics actually derives from the Greek word for household, *oikos*."

But if the household is like a firm, it's like one that could use some management consultants. We often make drastic miscalculations about the value of our time, taking a do-it-yourself

ILLUSTRATED BY ANNETTE MARIE PEARCY

approach to tasks that might be less costly in time and money to hire out. A simple car oil-change, for example, costs from £14.99 at Kwik-Fit. You won't find the supplies to do it yourself for much less, it's messy work and can take a couple of hours, and yet lots of us change our own oil.

Do the Maths

In the past, economists looked strictly at income to put a price on leisure hours. Now, the study of off-the-clock time—or "household production"—is getting a fresh look, taking into account factors such as satisfaction and pleasure. In 2000 the Government produced its first Time Use Survey, which included data on time spent by households on things like shopping, cleaning, washing dishes.

Academic papers with titles such as "Time v Goods: The Value of Measuring Household Technologies" are also circulating. Now that pinched budgets are forcing some people to work longer hours, it puts a higher premium on cost-effective use of free time.

Economists say one of the most common miscalculations is "outsourcing" child-care needs to free both parents to contribute to the household income. While plenty of parents work because they enjoy their jobs, others think they can't afford not to. Sometimes the maths proves otherwise, as Steve and Gaby Brown of Stoke Newington, London, discovered.

Gaby works full-time as a BBC producer and Steve had his own business as a freelance video director. When their third child arrived, the couple looked at what it was costing them to have both parents working— from the £12,000 in childcare to the £7,000 in extra taxes. By the time they threw in Steve's work-associated costs (high telephone bills, travel, convenience meals), they determined that if he gave up his job they would lose only a few hundred pounds a month. "Now I have more time, we're also managing our money better," says Steve. "And as a family we are much happier."

Work or Fun?

Economists put household activities into two categories: consumption (things you enjoy) and production (anything that feels like work). Love cleaning the house? It's consumption. Hate cleaning? Then it's production, strengthening the argument in favour of paying someone else to do it.

It's not just about the money, says Gershuny. It's about whether we get pleasure from doing some of these chores, compared to the hassle of farming them out. "I get pleasure from weeding. It would be odd for me not to do the gardening just because I could spend that time earning more at my consultancy rates than I'd spend on hiring a gardener."

That's how Sarah Kalliney justifies her epic battle with the mobile phone company. It was worth it for the satisfaction. "These people are taking money that's not theirs," she explains. "If they're going to ruin my day, I'm going to ruin theirs." After tracking down the company director, she finally won her fight. The firm has since taken steps to improve its customer service.

In working out how to maximise time, salary is one jumping-off point. Calculate what an hour of your time is worth, based on your salary after taxes. Using that figure, compare the cost of doing the job yourself versus outsourcing it. If you do it yourself,

add in the price of any materials; if you employ someone else, factor in time taken to hire and manage them.

Next look at the non-financial costs and benefits. Consider how much you enjoy doing the job and what you're giving up. These conclusions will steer you in one direction or another.

To see how this formula works in

Should You Do It Yourself?

Here's a framework to help you decide:

What Is Your "Real" Time Salary?

1. Your monthly take-home pay, after taxes . . . . £_____
2. Hours you typically work in a month . . . . _____hours
3. Divide 1 by 2; this is your real time (hourly) salary . . . . £_____
4. Cost to hire someone else . . . . £_____
5. Time you would save, in hours, by hiring someone else . . . . _____hours
6. Costs of doing this job yourself (eg, buying supplies) . . . . £_____
7. Multiply 3 by 5 . . . . £_____
8. Add 6 and 7; this is the total cost of doing the task yourself . . . . £_____

Outcome: If 8 is less than 4, there is a strong financial case for doing the job yourself. If 8 is more than 4, there is a strong financial case for hiring someone else to do the work

Psychological Costs and Benefits

	strongly disagree			strongly agree	
	1	2	3	4	5
1. Psychological Benefits: I enjoy doing this task myself	1	2	3	4	5
2. Skill Premium: I could do this task as well as the person I'd hire	1	2	3	4	5
3. Opportunity Costs: If I do this task myself, I won't miss out on the other activities important to me	1	2	3	4	5
4. Indirect Rewards: If I do this task myself, I'll get other benefits such as exercise or self-confidence	1	2	3	4	5
SCORING: Add up your points					_____

Point System

4–8 Points: The psychological costs are high; outsource the task if you can afford to

9–12 Points: Let the financial calculations in the first part of this chart dictate your actions

13–20 Points: The psychological benefits are great; do the job yourself even if you can easily hire it out

OutSourcing

How much do you have to earn per year to make it worth paying someone to do these chores?

Ironing: **£7,000**

House cleaning: **£13,600**

Dog walking: **£16,500**

Gardening: **£19,000**

Paint house: **£27,500**

Car valet: **£37,000**

Food shopping: **£53,000**

Clean gutters: **£68,000**

Personal organiser: **£145,000**

JESSE SHAPIRO, NANCY TAFOYA, NEIL CARLSON

the real world, we outsourced some tasks then redid the jobs ourselves to compare. Buying a jar of pre-chopped garlic, for example, saved 22 minutes of slicing and dicing. According to the formula, anybody who makes more than £6,000 a year can afford it. The downside: fresh garlic tastes better.

Investing in technology—even a good garlic press—can change these calculations, as we found when faced with a new pair of suit trousers that needed turning up.

If you're all thumbs with a needle and thread then a sewing machine could speed up the job—and cut down on those pricked fingers and expletives! But if you loathe sewing and want the result to look professional, take the trousers to the dry cleaners. Many will do minor alterations. It'll be worth your while even if you earn as little as £8,000.

Many hard-core do-it-yourselfers are grappling with similar variables. Mark Berg, a financial planner, once rented a pneumatic drill to rip out his concrete basement floor. But the garage sale he held last summer challenged his can-do attitude. After hours of planning and a long day in the sun, he netted a nasty sunburn and a wage of £2.37 an hour—somewhat short of the £120 an hour he charges at the office.

"We will never do another garage sale again," he says.

Which jobs do you do yourself? And which do you outsource? Write to the address on page 10 or e-mail YouSaidIt@readersdigest.co.uk.

YOU'VE GOT TO BE KIDDING

Children are a lot like pancakes. You sort of spoil the first one and you get better at it the second time round. By the third one, you flip it over just at the right time. KELLY RIPA, actress

We asked our son if he wanted a little brother or sister. He replied, "No, thank you, Mummy." CATHERINE ZETA-JONES

LAUGHTER, THE BEST MEDICINE

TRAVELLING THROUGH the desert, the two Englishmen saw a mirage on the horizon.

In front of them was a bustling market brimming with bowls of custard, jelly, sponge, cream and hundreds and thousands.

"How odd," said one man.

"Yes," nodded the other. "It's a trifle bazaar."

JO PAGE, Melton, Suffolk

JIM'S DOCTOR tells him he has only one day to live.

When Jim goes home to share the bad news with his wife, she asks what he wants to do with the little bit of time he has left.

"All I want", Jim tells his beloved wife, "is to spend my last few hours reliving our honeymoon." Which is exactly what they did.

But after four hours of blissful romance, she announces that she's tired and wants to go to sleep.

"Oh, come on," Jim whispers in her ear.

"Look," his wife snaps, "I've got to get up in the morning. You haven't!"

THE BLIND MAN walks into a bar and says, "Want to hear a blonde joke?"

The barman tells him, "Well, I'm blond and I won't appreciate it. The man sitting next to you is 18 stone and is also blond. The man behind you is 20 stone and he's a blond too. Do you still want to tell it?"

"No way," says the blind man. "Not if I have to explain it three times!"

PAT PATEL

ST PETER greets a man at the Pearly Gates. "What have you done to deserve entry into heaven?" he asks.

"Well, on my trip to the Black Hills, I came upon a gang of bikers threatening a young woman," says the man. "So I went up to the biggest,

Bless you!

Reynolds

received this letter. "Dear Dad, Don't dig up the garden! That's where I buried the *bodies*. Love, Walter."

The next morning, a group of policemen stormed the property and dug up the entire garden.

They didn't find any bodies, though, so they apologised to the old man and left.

Soon the farmer received another letter. It read: "Dear Dad, You can go ahead and plant the potatoes now. It's the best I could do under the circumstances. Love, Walter."

toughest biker and punched him in the nose. Then I kicked over his bike, yanked his ponytail and ripped out his nose ring. When I had finished with him, I turned to the rest of the gang and said, 'Leave this woman alone or you'll have to answer to me!'"

St Peter was impressed. "When did this happen?"

"Just a couple of minutes ago," said the man.   E.T. THOMPSON

An OLD MAN living alone on a farm wrote to his only son Walter, in prison.

"Dear Walter, I'm feeling bad because it looks like I won't be able to plant my potato garden this year. I'm just getting too old to be digging up a garden plot. I wish you were here—I know you would take care of it for me. Love, Dad."

About a week later, the farmer

Dave's about to go on his first ever holiday and is feeling a little apprehensive. So he phones the airline and asks, "How long does it take to fly from London to Alicante?"

"Just a minute," says the agent.

"Thanks," Dave responds, and hangs up.   LINDA OUELLETTE

Knock, knock, knock. A man opens the door and finds a snail on his porch. He picks it up and throws it as far as he can.

Three years later, three more knocks. The man opens the door and there sits the same snail. He looks at the man and says, "What was that about?"   DREW CAREY, Dirty Jokes and Beer

---

For a daily dose of humour, visit "Laughfinder" at www.readersdigest.co.uk

Ferragamo's Gift

My mother—and a famous shoe designer—taught me that anything is possible | BY SUSAN SHREVE

WANDERING around the shops, my daughters and I stop to look at shoes wherever we go. This is their choice, these women who as little girls teetered round the house balancing like cranes in my mother's high heels. I sit and wait while they try on shoe after shoe, readjusting their positions in the mirror, eyes downcast, considering their feet.

"So?" one of them will ask me. "What do you think of these?"

"I love them." I say this about every pair, of course. Which isn't true. I have a complicated relationship with shoes. Given a choice—which a mother of two daughters on a shopping spree doesn't necessarily have—I'd never go into a shoe shop at all.

But my mother would be ecstatic. In the romance of shoes, they are my mother's daughters.

I am her true daughter—and growing up, I was her full-time job, one she took on with grace. I'd had polio as a baby and learned to walk in calipers wearing heavy, brown orthopaedic

He made shoes
for Audrey Hepburn, Marilyn Monroe—and me

lace-ups. The fact that they were not the black patent shoes the other little girls were wearing concerned me less than it did my mother, who was in love with footwear.

There was an element of boot camp to my childhood: posture exercises, ballet school run by a French dancer who wasn't enthusiastic at the arrival of a hopeful ballerina wearing clumpy shoes and a caliper. Mother bought me ballet slippers. I couldn't walk in them. But I held tight to the barre, pretending I could leap, my legs in perfect half-moons, my pink slippers pointed.

By the time I was seven, my mother had moved on to tennis, which she decided I could play while wearing black rain shoes over my lace-ups. And long before anyone in my class had heard of ballroom dancing, my mother played swing music on the phonograph in the living room, took me in her arms and taught me how.

By 12, after a series of operations, I could walk unaided. When I turned 15, she signed me up for dancing school with boys. She took me shopping in the sales, buying me a slip-like dress with a deep V and a strapless satiny thing. But shoes were a dilemma: I wore two sizes, one 5½, the other 3.

"I can't possibly wear these to dancing school," I said of my orthopaedics.

"Of course not," mother agreed. "We'll buy you heels."

So we bought a pair of size 5½, stuffing one shoe with loo paper so it would fit my smaller foot.

I wore the satiny dress to the first dance. I managed to take a turn with a boy so tall I couldn't see his face—which was just as well, since the loo paper began to trail in a long ribbon across the dance floor. I fled and hid in the ladies' room—my feet up on the lavatory seat so no one could see I was there—until dancing school was over. I never went back.

"We'll find you shoes," my mother promised me that night.

"I don't need to go to dances," I said.

"Maybe not," she answered. "But you need to have the shoes, in case you change your mind."

Somewhere in my mother's fashion-magazine reading, she recalled that Salvatore Ferragamo had a child with polio. She wrote to him, saying that she, too, had such a child, telling him the story of the dance. Would he consider making my shoes?

By this time, Ferragamo was well

known as a shoemaker, with rich clients all over the world. But my mother was certain he would write back. And he did, inviting us to Florence, offering to make a "last"—a model of my foot—at no cost.

Ferragamo died before we could get to Florence. As it turned out, he did not have a child with polio. But he was a sympathetic man and his wife and daughters honoured his letter.

And so it was that as an awkward, self-conscious teenager, I sat at the Palazzo Spini Feroni headquarters next to my lovely mother and was measured. What I remember about that afternoon—besides the slender models walking the marble floors and the elegant women sampling the wares—is the sense I had of my mother. She commanded the room in her quiet way, as if she had brought to Florence a precious treasure, a jewel of such particularity that for a moment I lost myself and believed her.

For the next ten years—until the building where the lasts were housed burned down—I'd scan magazines with my mother, looking for shoes. I'd send the pictures to Ferragamo's and, for the equivalent of £20 a pair, I'd get the most amazing creations: olive-green suede with an orange leaf, grey leather with a black heel like an umbrella, my wedding shoes, with seed pearls in the shape of a butterfly. They weren't exactly right for a young woman in the shoeless 1960s. But they were beautiful.

My mother was a quiet, mysterious woman of understated elegance. When she died, I discovered in her wardrobe shelves of shoes, the price tags still attached. Suddenly I could see her in the shoe department; arthritis had made it impossible for her to wear the slender high heels and strappy sandals she adored. But she would buy them anyway, pretending she was going to a dance.

She believed that anything is possible in life and that she should always be ready for surprises—a philosophy she had taught me with the full measure of her love.

NATURE CALLS

One of California's state parks, the Jedediah Smith Park, has a beautiful redwood forest. The magnificent trees can grow over 350 feet high and measure as much as 16 feet in diameter. I was at a campsite enjoying the stillness and beauty of my surroundings, thinking how the park had the feel of a giant cathedral, when a camper van  pulled up next to me. The driver stuck his head out of the window and shouted, "Is there anything to see here besides trees?" BRUCE JOHNSTON

Call of the

If you think animal art means tacky portraits of pets or flying ducks on the wall, think again

Ever since she was a little girl growing up in London and making regular trips to Regent's Park zoo, Kendra Haste has been fascinated with the way wild animals move and behave. Ten years ago, in the final year of her degree in illustration at the Camberwell College of Arts, she was frustrated by the commercial graphic design emphasis of the course. So she decided to turn her love of animals into art. Spending hours observing rhinos, tigers and chimps in their zoo enclosures, Kendra made vivid, detailed charcoal and chalk sketches. But she wanted to capture each animal's spirit and energy in three-dimensional form. Artists have traditionally sculpted

KENT MICHAELS

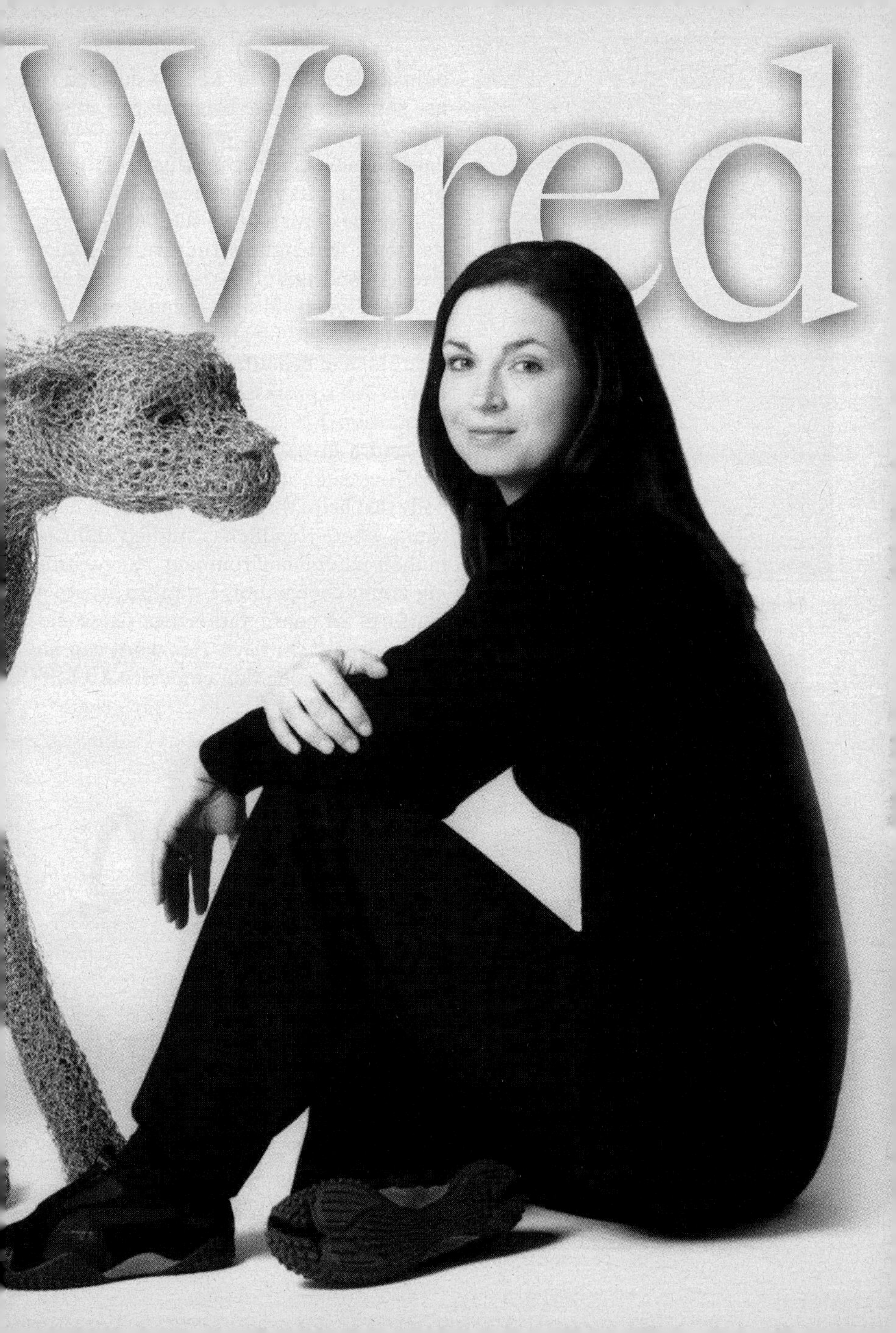
Wired

Mandrill (2001). The distinctive nose is made from paper pulp. Monkeys' complex social interaction (below) make them one of Kendra's favourite subjects

animals from bronze. Kendra decided to use something more original: galvanised wire. After months of work—and raw, bandaged hands—she began to perfect the art of moulding its fibrous texture into the semblance of fur and muscle, while using its dense-but-light structure to evoke strength and agility.

The 32-year-old's life-sized sculptures fetch up to £25,000 and have been called "truthful and beautiful" by the Royal College of Art's professor of natural history illustration, John Norris Wood.

Kendra gives a share of her sales to charities such as the Tusk Trust, a UK body that helps threatened species in Tanzania, where Kendra has studied animals in their natural environment. "By recording animal behaviour, I want to create a platform for conservation awareness and fund-raising," she says. Her work can be seen at the London Contemporary Art Fair, January 14–18.   SIMON HEMELRYK

BLACK AND WHITE PHOTOGRAPHY DONATED BY KENT MICHAELS

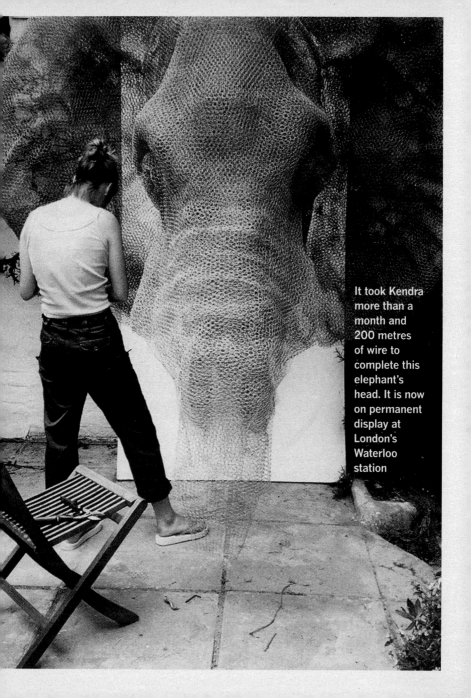

It took Kendra more than a month and 200 metres of wire to complete this elephant's head. It is now on permanent display at London's Waterloo station

the BOY who loved windows

My autistic son lived in his own world. I would try anything to bring him back into mine

BY PATRICIA STACEY

FROM THE MOMENT our son Walker was born, we knew something was different about him. Friends tried to convince us we were wrong and no one at our local health centre would believe us. But we had no doubt. By the time he was six months old, he struggled to breathe at night, he flailed in space, he could barely grab a toy. Mysteriously, he would look at us only when we stood far above him or across the room.

Finally my husband Cliff and I went to a paediatrician near where we live, in Amherst, Massachusetts. The doctor measured our baby in all possible ways, checking length, reflexes, muscle tone. Then he tried talking to him. "Walker," he said. Walker didn't respond. The doctor waved a fuzzy red ball. "Walker!" "Walker!" he said, first firmly, then animatedly, and finally shouting. Walker lay staring out of the window, impassive, ineluctably drawn to the light.

Gently, the doctor explained that we

needed to prepare ourselves for the limitations of our son's abilities. Walker might never walk or talk; he might even be severely mentally disabled. We decided it was time to call REACH, a local early-intervention programme.

Walker's diagnosis was sensory integration disorder, a condition characterised by heightened sensitivity to a variety of stimuli. His case was assigned to Arlene Spooner, a physiotherapist with training in this field.

On the day that Arlene met Walker,

he wasn't the listless baby he'd been at the paediatrician's. In fact, he appeared electrified, a caricature of excitement. His head swung from side to side; he laughed constantly, almost maniacally; his arms and legs moved rapidly, as if he were sprinting through the air.

Arlene studied Walker with obvious alarm; then she chose her words carefully: "You have a very sensitive son."

Cliff looked up "sensory integration disorder" on the Internet and found it was cross-referenced with autism. No one had actually used the term, but Arlene had expressed concern at Walker's unrelatedness, his tendency to pull inward, the peculiar motions of his limbs.

PEOPLE WITH autism, Cliff and I learned, are often not out of tune with this world but, ironically, far too aware of it. The world is too much with them and because they are excruciatingly sensitive, they're forced to retreat.

Imagine your sensory world scrambled and unregulated, your auditory intake a rock station—or worse, mere static blasting incessantly in your ears. Imagine your kitchen light as bright as a searchlight, boring into your cornea every time you turned it on. Imagine your clothes so irritating they seem lined with metal scraping brushes. Imagine fumes in a restaurant so overpowering you think the cook must be boiling Mace. This can be the world of the autistic.

Most experts agree autism has a genetic component. But the possibility that additional factors are at work— toxins from pesticides, other chemicals or vaccines—has also been debated. [Currently in the UK, some 500,000 people have been diagnosed as suffering from autism.]

ARLENE BEGAN WORKING with Walker in a darkened room. No matter how we altered his position, his head always moved to the light like the needle of a compass. But in dim light, with shades drawn, Walker slowly moved his head away from the window. Still, what he looked at was not us but objects. Toys.

"Why objects?" I asked Arlene.

"Because faces have an amazing amount of information in them," she said. "Especially the eyes. Right now, that's too much information for him."

One day Arlene asked me to curl Walker tightly in a ball and hold him close in my arms. "Now try to get his attention," she said, "but don't smile much. That would be hard for him."

I held him firmly and waited. He looked up at me, and his large, round green eyes penetrated mine. Suddenly his hand rose to touch my face. I shivered—he was seven months old and had never come this close before. But in an instant his hand flew in the other direction and his eyes turned away as if looking at me had been painful.

"It's not that he doesn't want to," Arlene said. "It's that he can't."

TO HELP WITH WALKER, Arlene brought in specialist Dawn Smith. Dawn had never seen a child so young with symptoms of autism—usually the disorder becomes apparent at 18 months to two years of age, when speech and social skills are slow to develop.

One of the most common ways to treat an autistic child is behaviour modification: asking the child to perform a task (putting an ice cube in a bucket, for example), and then rewarding him for completing the task. The idea is to teach the child to adopt

Walker was fascinated with objects. Faces held too much information

more socially correct behaviours.

But Dawn had reservations about using a behavioural approach in Walker's case; it didn't address the crucial issue of emotional development. By a fortunate coincidence, she was primed to try a new technique.

Dawn had just read an article by child psychiatrist Stanley Greenspan and his colleague Serena Wieder. The two had developed something called "floor time"—combining occupational and speech therapy, and a technique referred to as "circles of communication". A circle is started when someone—a parent or therapist—tries to engage the child, and completed when that someone receives a response. Smile and the baby smiles back: one circle. Hand a toy to the baby and the baby hands it back: another circle.

Using this approach, Greenspan had helped more than 50 per cent of his 200 patients to become fully functioning children—warm, engaged, interactive, verbal and creative. Another 30 per cent made substantial progress.

I called Greenspan, who, though difficult to see, was eager to work with Walker because of his age. We met him in Bethesda, Maryland.

Over years of study, psychologists

Is My Baby OK?

SOON AFTER Marcel Bujnowski was born, his mother knew there was a problem. But the doctor told her the baby was simply colicky. Nine months later, Marcel couldn't control his head, sit up or hold an object. The diagnosis was cerebral palsy.

His parents had him in occupational, speech and physiotherapy just two weeks later. Now seven years old, Marcel plays the piano, speaks English and Polish, and skis with a special walker.

When parents suspect something is not right with their child, they should act on their instincts as the Bujnowskis did. A gut feeling can be more accurate than a medical diagnosis.

And parents should not accept a wait-and-see approach. Doctors are making strides in early diagnosis and intervention for children with conditions such as cerebral palsy, autism, Down's syndrome and hearing loss.

"The infant brain is so elastic", says cerebral palsy expert Dr Murray Goldstein, "that the probability of success is greater the earlier the intervention."

MELANIE HOWARD in BabyTalk Magazine

had noted that autistic children could not do anything imaginative or conceptually abstract. They seem hopelessly mired in the literal, unable to feel sympathy for others or understand others' thought processes.

Why? Greenspan asked himself. The answer was staring him in the face. Or, rather, in all those young faces that simply couldn't look him in the eye.

Greenspan and his colleagues realised that autistic children wouldn't understand abstractions until they understood their own emotions. As a child develops, everything he does and thinks is largely because of emotions. The autistic child was missing a clear understanding of himself—a connection among feelings, actions and ideas. He couldn't leap into a conceptual world beyond himself because he didn't "get" himself.

During our first meeting with Greenspan, he videotaped Cliff and me playing with Walker, now 11 months old. He called out orders, telling us to work harder and faster and be more engaging, more intimate. "No, no, no...now you've lost him." When we'd finally captured our son's attention for longer periods, he'd shout out, "Now you're cookin'!"

We had to make Walker work for whatever he wanted. "You must become the button that makes anything he wants happen," Greenspan said.

That evening Cliff and I were in a restaurant with Walker. "I'll give you this cup", I said, "if you squeeze my finger." Walker didn't react. We weren't sure he'd even understood. I said it again. This time the boy who had never before responded to a verbal request put his hand up to mine and squeezed.

DOING FLOOR TIME, I often felt I was performing a desperate sort of stand-up comedy to save my son's life. Not only were sessions exhausting—we found ourselves clapping, jumping up and down, making up songs—but our voices had to be ever livelier, the games more enticing, the joking more exaggerated.

Children such as Walker are inclined to recede to an internal landscape that is far more seductive than the "real" world. That's why Greenspan told us we must maintain Walker's attention and help him to "build" himself—block by block, through each phase of development, physical and emotional.

One day when Walker was nearly a year old, Dawn, Arlene and I were all on the floor with him. We had taught him to crawl at about ten months, but he still couldn't sit up, a skill his peers had mastered at six months. Seeing that he was trying, we cheered him on. And when he succeeded, we clapped. This physical leap spurred a social one as well—Walker looked from Dawn to me to Arlene as if to say, "Hey, you guys, did you see me?"

THE RESULTS of floor time were staggering. Walker's expressiveness grew, as did all his motor skills. Emotion bloomed on his face. He exhibited a sense of humour. He laughed during our games, toyed with us, made up his own ways of playing.

In May 2000, when Walker was nearly four, Greenspan, who'd been closely following our son's progress, told us he was doing wonderfully by any standard. "He's a great problem solver, a creative thinker, has a can-do attitude. More important, he's got that spark in his eye."

Today Walker is a warm, intelligent, engaged schoolboy, who occasionally has his unruly moments. Most important, he has a deep sense of empathy. When his great-aunt died, he worried that her surviving sister would be lonely. How often do little boys put themselves in someone else's place? Perhaps this high degree of emotional intelligence—a gift, really—is related to his inherent sensitivity.

My experience with Walker has taught me that early human interaction is the starting point of all knowledge. We can be complete, conscious beings only when we have known ourselves through the eyes of another.

———————

Patricia Stacey writes about her son's recovery in "The Boy Who Loved Windows" (Perseus Publishing, £15).

'ARMLESS ANTICS

Twice in one day, Steven Richard King tried to rob a bank armed with only his finger. In the first attempt, King stuffed his hand into his shirt and told employees it was a gun. That worked well until the "gun" slipped from his shirt. The man then crossed the street and tried again. He was promptly shown the door by bank officials. ERIC MBOGORI

Bloody But Beautiful

After centuries of conflict, this idyllic island retreat still stands proud | BY ROBERT WERNICK

"I N CORSICA," said the petrol-station attendant, "we give directions more often in terms of up and down than of left and right. If you want to see the country, go along the coast in either direction and when you get the chance, go up."

Corsica is a 3,360-square-mile fist of fractured rock, some of it rising straight out of the sea, some of it towering more than 8,500 feet high. I was negotiating one of the more spectacular hairpin bends when a sizeable herd of pigs ambled across the road to gnaw at some undergrowth.

"That's the way it's always been in Corsica," said a man at the village restaurant where I had lunch. "We let our domestic animals run wild, with nothing but a tag pinned to their ears to let everyone know who they belong to."

He then told us to try the Corsican sausage. "There's nothing like its taste anywhere," he added. "It comes from the plants the pigs eat." He was referring to the *maquis*, the dense scrub land that covers half the island and suffuses it with a bittersweet smell.

The sausage was indeed delicious, and it led the talk to an item in the paper about a man arrested for shooting two of his neighbour's pigs for chewing up the flowers in his garden. The restaurant owner was indignant that the French government, which had feloniously bought his island a mere 234 years ago, should be interfering in the private affairs of two Corsicans.

"What I don't understand", said my dining companion, "is why did that man shoot the pigs? Why didn't he shoot the *neighbour*?"

He was half smiling, but a generation ago, the law of the vendetta was still going strong. "Vendetta" is practically the only Corsican word to have passed without change into most of the world's dictionaries. The vendetta code states that an assault on a family's honour must be repaid in blood, and that blood repaid in turn until one or both of the families are exterminated.

"THERE WAS one moment when we were the only truly free people in the world. And it was all thanks to that man," the restaurateur reminisced. He gestured to a portrait of a sturdy man in an old-fashioned uniform. "The father of his country," he said. "Pasquale Paoli."

In 1752, Paoli called on the families of Corsica to throw out the forces of the Most Serene Republic of Genoa, which had ruled the island for almost 200 years. In 1755 Paoli created an independent republic with a democratic constitution. Alas, it lasted just 14 years. The Genoese, still entrenched in a few coastal areas, sold the island to the government of King Louis XV. (France had always wanted a secure naval base in the Mediterranean.) Paoli was defeated in battle; he'd eventually die in exile in London. Since 1769 the

MAP BY 5W INFOGRAPHICS

Hillside villages such as Sainte Lucie de Tallano provide a glimpse of rural Corsican life

island has remained a part of France.

The island's isolated communities and tightly knit clans remained long after the French had introduced maps and paved roads. Little by little, though, the splendid isolation was eroded by modern inventions and modern wars. With the dawning of relatively cheap air fares in the 1970s, the rate of change became torrential. Today the island devotes most of its economy to cosseting some two million tourists who visit the laid-back picturesque land each year. And for its 260,000 inhabitants, tourism has meant a massive inflow of cash, drugs, traffic and satellite dishes.

Yet the pastoral life lives on. In fact, once you leave the narrow strips of coastal plain, there are no advertising hoardings, no supermarkets, no garages,

no tall buildings. Up in the mountains in summer you will still find shepherds and goatherds with their flocks.

But long gone are what the maquis was most famous for in the old days: bandits, which in Corsica is not necessarily a term of reproach. Like Robin Hood, many Corsican bandits were seen as heroic resisters of alien oppression. In the trackless tangle of the maquis, bandits were safe from the authorities.

COMING DOWN from the mountains to Corsica's biggest town, Ajaccio, you have to cross the roaring Liamone River, where, in 1769, a decisive event in Corsican and French history took place. Among the Corsican patriots fleeing the battlefield where Paoli's cause was lost for ever were his personal secretary—Carlo Buona-parte—and his pregnant young wife Letizia, who three months later gave birth to her second son Napoleon.

Had Napoleon been born a few years earlier, he might well have grown up a Genoese general. As it was, he was born a Frenchman, and his father managed to wangle a scholarship for little Napoleon to a French military school—the first rung on the ladder to his becoming the greatest French general of all time. And it was Napoleon who made Corsica a part of the centralised French state.

The arrangement has given the Corsicans more years of peace than they've known since the fall of the Roman Empire. It's also allowed them to leave their poverty-stricken shores and make a living in the French army or government or business. Or in organised crime, where the mythology of the French underworld is as full of Corsicans as America's is of Sicilians.

Although most Corsicans speak French, there has been a determined resurrection of the Corsican language, now taught in schools, as well as a revival of the old polyphonic music and ancient handicrafts. And, like other peripheral outposts, Corsica has also seen the rise of revolutionary groups demanding a return to a highly romanticised past. During a demonstration in 1975 against French farmers from Algeria who were given land earmarked for Corsican farmers, two policemen were killed, setting off a wave of sporadic shootings and bombings that has sputtered along ever since.

Perhaps a hopeful augury can be found in the village of Cargèse, on a beautiful cliff-bound bay on the west coast. Here, hundreds of years ago, several hundred Greeks were brought by the Genoese from the mountains of Greece. Separated by religion and language, Greeks and Corsicans shot at each other and burned down each other's houses. Gradually, they agreed to live side by side, but their lives remained compartmentalised. They went to separate churches, avoiding contact in daily life.

But as the years lengthened into centuries, the old hatreds subsided. Though the residents of Cargèse still worship apart, they speak Corsican and French, and shop, eat and do business together.

Today that business is mostly tourism. When I passed through Cargèse, people from a dozen countries chatted in cafes and headed for the beaches. Two churches stood on neighbouring hills, doors open to all. There was not a gun in sight.

LITERAL-MINDED

I was horrified to find my son eating out of the sugar bowl. "Don't let me catch you doing that again," I scolded. My boy was willing, but dubious. "I'll try, Mummy," he told me, "but you walk so quietly sometimes!"   PAT BEVANS

Worried by NHS waiting times?

Thought you couldn't afford private health insurance?

HealthNow is a new kind of private health insurance. It focuses on conditions for which there are likely to be long NHS waiting times. So it costs substantially less than you'd expect. In fact, you can enjoy all of the benefits of HealthNow from as little as £9.95 a month – that's less than 33p a day, depending on your age.

Fast consultations, fast diagnosis, fast treatment

HealthNow gives you fast access to a consultant for diagnosis and then quality private treatment for

Here's a new kind of plan which costs substantially less than you'd expect

conditions such as heart bypasses, hip replacements, cataracts, slipped discs, hernias and so on. So you don't have the worry of waiting for a diagnosis. And you don't have to put your life on hold while you wait for treatment.

For your free Information Pack, call us free now.

A SELECTION OF OUR LOW MONTHLY PREMIUMS

From 33p a day

Age of eldest insured	Just you	You and your spouse or partner	You and your children	Whole family
18-24	£9.95	£17.11	£22.48	£29.10
50-54	£26.04	£50.82	£38.07	£62.81
75-79	£60.48	£117.32	£69.32	£129.31

Cover is available if you are aged 18-79 and renewable up to age 85.
Cover ceases on your 85th birthday. Includes 5% Insurance Premium Tax.

HEALTH *NOW*

NO WAITING FOR TREATMENT
NO EXCESSES TO PAY
NO WAITING TO SEE A CONSULTANT

Reader's Digest Financial Services

0800 028 0050

CALL FREE MONDAY - FRIDAY 8am - 8pm,
SATURDAY - SUNDAY 9am - 5pm

Quote ref: 1698

or alternatively, tick the box on the Reader Information Service coupon within this magazine.

A grey drizzly morning, a school bus on its rounds, a sudden flash flood

BY LEE MAYNARD

FIVE-YEAR-OLD Tammara Vana could not stand still. She fussed with her wavy brown hair as her mother tried to brush it. It was school photo day at the Valley Mills school and Tammara wanted to look her best.

In crisp shirts and fresh jeans, Tammara's brothers waited in the living room. Scott, a lanky 11-year-old, was at the window playing lookout, watching for the school bus while his little brother Joshua, four years younger, sat on the couch engrossed in cartoons on TV.

Rain had been pounding the rolling Texas hill country for weeks, smothering pastures, sluicing through gullies, swelling creeks. In the 24 hours before dawn on February 16, another inch and a half had fallen.

AT 6.30AM, Art Aguilar slowly eased the huge, empty school bus along muddy Granger Road. It was raining lightly as he approached his first pick-up. He touched the brakes and eased to a stop in front of a white ranch house. The Vanas were new to the area; this would be

High and dry today, the Vana children peer through the bus's escape hatch

only the second week they'd taken the bus. All three were good kids, no trouble at all.

AT 6.35 SCOTT SAW the lights of the bus. Joshua grabbed his coat and Tammara leaned away from the last swipe of her mother's comb. In seconds, the children were moving down the dark drive and up the metal steps of the empty bus. Scott ambled to the rear and draped himself across the long

the bus a few feet away. The headlights flared in a bright fan across a dark belt of water some 60 feet wide, completely covering the crossing. Having driven a bus for eight years, Aguilar had seen this many times before. At roughly 12 tons, the vehicle shouldn't have any trouble with a few inches of water.

Settling back in his seat, he shifted into low gear and crawled on to the crossing. The heavy bus moved easily through the water. The other side was

The kids were screaming. Aguilar clung to his seat as the bus rolled

back seat. It was his habit to nap during the hour-long trip to school. Joshua and Tammara sat talking near the front, their laughter rising and falling.

About two miles from the Vanas' house, the road dipped sharply to a low-water crossing at Childress Creek. Crossings such as these are common in the Texas hill country. They're simply built-up roadbeds across streams that are trickles most of the year.

This morning Childress Creek was running faster and higher than usual. Just to be cautious, Aguilar stopped

less than a bus-length away. *No problem*, he thought.

But then, almost instantly, water was over the tyres, lapping against the school lettering. The rear of the bus slipped on the algae-covered concrete. In seconds it was loose on the flood, floating back into the darkness.

THE VANA CHILDREN were screaming. Aguilar clung to his seat as the bus rolled deeply to the right as if trying to dump him out of the door. If it rolled all the way over, they were dead.

Frigid water surged inside. Scott leapt from the back seat to help his brother and sister, trainers splashing in the water that was swooshing up the aisle. Joshua and Tammara jumped on to their seats. "Mum!" Joshua screamed. Scott realised he was screaming too.

Aguilar wrestled himself from behind the steering wheel. The children were on the edge of panic, their frightened voices cutting through the sound of the rushing water.

"Stay steady! Stay in your seats," Aguilar called as he waded towards them. "I just need you to calm down."

To his relief, the children grew quiet and scrambled up to stand on the vinyl-covered benches. Water swirled up to the seat cushions.

The lumbering bus floated backwards downstream until it lodged on a submerged gravel bar. Debris-laden water rolled up against the heavy grille and gushed through cracks in the closed doors, forcing its way through the bus.

Aguilar grabbed the mobile phone from beside the driver's seat and punched in the emergency number. But inside the bus, he got only static. "Go to the back!" he ordered. The rear of the bus was not quite as badly submerged as the rest. The creek, now a river, roared past outside.

Aguilar feared that the water would fill the bus. Then he remembered the roof hatch situated in the middle of the bus. He stood on a seat and cranked it open. Gently he picked up Tammara—her shiny pink coat was slippery in his hands. "When you get up on top, stay still," he told her. Carefully he stood back up on the seat and lifted the tiny girl through the hatch.

Scott helped Aguilar boost Joshua out and then grabbed the edge of the hatch and scrambled through himself. The driver took a quick look round—the bus was half full of water. He struggled through the tight opening.

On top, he was stunned. The bus was an island in a torrent 200 feet wide. It was no longer raining here; the danger came from upstream. Debris and trees ripped from the banks hurtled by like torpedoes.

Aguilar tried the phone again. Outside the bus, the call went through.

"What is your location?" the operator asked and then immediately sent out a call to the sheriff's department.

Now they had to wait—clothes soaked, shivering in the wind on the cold, slick metal roof. Tammara's neatly brushed hair was ruined, and she was worried that the schoolwork in her backpack was ruined too. "It's school photo day," she said quietly. "I'm going to be late."

Joshua's imagination was working overtime. He envisioned alligators in the water, a plunging waterfall waiting for them downstream.

Aguilar tried to reassure them, but the water was still rising. He estimated the stream to be 300 feet wide. And they could feel the bus moving beneath them.

To Aguilar's relief, Texas state troopers and the local firemen began to arrive. But it was soon clear they'd be unable to get to the bus—no one had fast-water rescue training or the right equipment. Men stood helplessly on both banks. All they were able to do was get a rope to the bus and send over life jackets.

Frustrated, the firemen developed a worst-case plan. If the children slipped or the bus rolled, dumping

off the roof, Mitchell thought. Quickly he radioed the people on the ground to get them back inside.

AT FIRST Aguilar's hope soared—then came word from the rescuers on the shore that they would have to go back down into the bus until the crew could lower a line.

Aguilar dropped through the hatch,

Derek Mitchell's Black Hawk created a storm of its own

them into the water, they would have men on ropes downstream dive in and try to catch them before they were swept away.

IN THE DISTANCE, Derek Mitchell swung his seven ton Black Hawk helicopter low out of the mist. Because the county had no chopper capable of a hoist-line rescue, officials had called for an army team from nearby Fort Hood. Though the rain had stopped, Mitchell's Black Hawk created a storm of its own—a 110mph downdraught that bent trees and sent mud and gravel flying.

We're going to blow those kids right

landing in icy water. Scott and Joshua lowered Tammara to him. Next Joshua swung inside. Once again they stood on the seats—this time with water up their legs. Soaked and cold, they waited for the chopper to get into position.

SIXTY FEET ABOVE, the Black Hawk buffeted the bus with its downdraught. Then there was a thump on the roof.

Aguilar looked up and saw a wet face. He lifted Tammara into the man's outstretched hands.

Trees alongside the creek made manoeuvring the chopper precarious. A gust of wind blew the soldier and the little girl into the limbs, ensnaring them. But the pilot and the hoist operator deftly extracted the pair, and landed them safely in a nearby field.

Mitchell's team made each rescue faster. Joshua was next. It took less than a minute to retrieve Scott. As he rose into the damp air, he looked down at Aguilar and gave him a thumbs-up.

Alone, the threatening rush of water all around him, Aguilar nevertheless experienced the biggest feeling of relief he'd ever known—the children were safe. Shortly the Black Hawk returned and pulled him out of the half-sunken wreck.

Aguilar held it all together telling the authorities what had happened. It was only in the privacy of the ambulance that he began to cry.

Afterwards, the Vana boys thought their ride on the rescue line was awesome. And though she was disappointed to have missed the photo day, Tammara had something no one else in her nursery class had—her picture on TV.

Art Aguilar is back in the driver's seat. His experience has convinced him of something awesome too—the responsibility anyone who works with children has. "Don't ever take it for granted," he says, "because you never know what's going to happen."

LOW-TECH MAN

P. J. O'Rourke: "Lack of romance is my real objection to writing on a computer. I decided to be a writer when Hemingway and Faulkner (and Mickey Spillane) were still lighting the literary sky. I was going to be a hard-drinking guy, tough but sensitive, in my old tweed jacket, pounding out truths on my Royal portable typewriter.

And how did those old-time writers get their tweed jackets to wear out at the elbows so they could have cool leather patches? Mine wear out because I spill ketchup on them. Also, tweed jackets ride up on the back of my neck when I'm writing and itch. Which brings me to the honest confession of why I don't use a computer—like the tweed jackets, I can't get it to work."

The New York Times

FOUR'S A CROWD

I was reminiscing with a friend about holidays. Recalling a day trip I had taken with three other people, I was frustrated at being able to name only two of my fellow tourists.

"Oh, never mind the third," I said to my friend. "It was probably someone unimportant." After a silence my friend said, "It was me."

LORAINE RICHARDSON, East Herrington, Tyne and Wear

ROOF PROBLEMS?

SAVE 20% NOW

SOLVED

Why Choose the Warmroof System?

- Creates a Warm, Dry, Clean Loft Space
- Fraction of the cost of our re-roofing
- Stops Slates and Tiles Slipping
- Stops Entry on Wind Driven Rain/Snow
- Eliminates Freezing Pipes
- Insulates - Saving fortunes on Heat Loss
- First Shown on Tomorrows World 1977

The Warmroof Under-Spray system locks slates and tiles in place, permanently sealing your roof to create a warm, dry, clean usable loftspace - waterproof for life.

Please arrange a FREE no obligation survey ☐
I would like further information ☐
Name: ....
Tel: ....
Address: ....
.... Postcode: ....
FREEPOST, Warmroof National Roofing Centre, BH8 8J

No Stamp Required

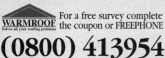

WARMROOF
Solves all your roofing problems

For a free survey complete the coupon or FREEPHONE

(0800) 413954

This Test Could Save Your Life

Are you at risk from a **silent killer?**

BY ELIZABETH ADLAM

N O CLIMB was too dangerous for Tony Ward. A mountaineering instructor from Ambleside in Cumbria, he'd led expeditions to the world's highest slopes. At 31, he was superbly fit.

Then he began to experience cramps, joint pains and headaches. Tests for arthritis proved negative, but his GP found he had gout and raised blood pressure, so prescribed medication.

Two years later, in May 1998, a hospital blood test showed Ward had increased levels of creatinine—a chemical that indicates a build-up of waste products in the bloodstream. Tony Ward was told his kidneys were shutting down—irreversibly.

The words hit him like a sledgehammer. "This can't happen to me. I don't feel that ill," he protested.

"That's the way it is with kidney disease," the specialist explained sombrely. "People often feel fine until the condition is quite advanced."

Neither Ward nor his GP had recognised the warning signs—test results that revealed protein in his urine, often the first indicator of kidney

---

In co-operation with The National Kidney Research Fund

113

disease, and high blood pressure.

Six months later, Ward's joint pain, gout and water retention were so severe he could barely walk. He was put on dialysis. Now, every night he attaches a tube from a dialysis machine to a catheter surgically inserted into his peritoneum—the lining of the abdominal cavity. For ten hours his blood is cleansed of toxins.

He knows this can only be a temporary fix while he waits for a transplant. But he keeps himself busy, lecturing, writing, raising money for kidney charities.

For a long time Ward was angry. Had doctors not failed to pick up on the results of his urine tests, he may have learned of his disease much earlier and delayed—maybe even prevented—the need for dialysis and transplant.

There are thousands of cases such as Tony Ward's—patients unaware of their risk, now on dialysis. The good news is that the test doctors perform for the early detection of kidney disease can now be taken at home. Here's what you need to know about kidney disease and this life-saving test.

Silent Menace

To understand how people like Tony Ward can be blindsided by the news that they have kidney disease, it is important to understand how the kidneys function. The two bean-shaped organs, each about the size of a fist, house a filtering system that processes some 200 litres of blood—equivalent to 500 cans of soft drink—daily. Of that,

two litres are discarded as waste and sent to the bladder.

Most kidney diseases attack this system. Damaged kidneys continue to excrete urine, but filter out much less of the body's wastes, which accumulate, poisoning the body.

A telltale sign that the kidneys are in trouble is the presence of excess protein—one of the body's basic building blocks—in urine. Healthy kidneys retain protein and excrete waste products. But when the kidneys begin to deteriorate, they can no longer hold on to the essential protein properly. Sometimes they also discharge blood into the urine.

The kidneys perform a number of vital functions and when they become damaged, the whole body is affected. Blood vessels become constricted and blood pressure rises. The disease can affect the brain and muscles, and interferes with the blood's ability to clot. Severe anaemia is not uncommon.

"If kidney disease is left untreated, bones can literally start to soften," says Professor John Feehally, consultant nephrologist at Leicester General Hospital and senior medical adviser to The National Kidney Research Fund (NKRF). Because the kidneys are no longer getting rid of phosphorus, this causes calcium levels in the blood to decrease. As a result, the body produces a hormone (parathyroid) that works on the bones to draw out the needed calcium, seriously weakening those bones further.

We each need only one kidney to survive, but by having two, the body

Who's Most At Risk?

KIDNEY DISEASE can strike anyone, but some are more prone to the disease than others:

- People with high blood pressure
- Diabetics
- Anyone 65 or older
- People with a family history of renal or heart disease
- Anyone overweight, especially around the mid-section
- Afro-Caribbeans and South Asians

Simple Lifesaver

There is an easy way to detect the early warning signs of kidney disease: a test that measures the presence of protein in the urine. Produced by Wellbeing MET, the at-home test kit is available through the NKRF.

It works simply. Urine is collected in a clean container and three chemically treated plastic strips are dipped in the urine. If the protein strip changes colour in a way the instructions describe, excessive protein is present. (The other two strips test for the presence of blood and nitrites and are additional indicators for kidney disease and bacterial infection.)

One positive reading is no cause for panic. It may mean you've just exercised strenuously, have a temperature or a simple bladder infection that needs clearing up. Check with your GP, though, and take a second test a few weeks later. Persistent excess protein, or proteinuria, often points to a kidney problem.

Some people get screened for kidney disease during, say, a life insurance medical, or on changing their GP, but the test is not used routinely. "It's much underused," says Professor Feehally. He believes those at high risk, such as the elderly, should receive regular screening.

Certainly eight-year-old Delise Cassarino from Manchester could have been saved weeks of pain if she'd been tested. Around Easter 2000, Delise started being violently sick. Two and a half years earlier, she'd had a

has a built-in savings account. As parts of both kidneys shut down, the healthy parts compensate. Eventually the body's reserves are depleted.

"Often patients have no warning," says Feehally. "They may have felt unwell for only a few days—then they're told they have kidney failure and will need dialysis the next day. It can be devastating."

As many as a quarter of a million Britons may have some form of kidney disease without realising it, and are completely unaware of their risk. Some 37,000 patients currently have end-stage renal failure and receive lifesaving treatments. It costs £145,000 for just one patient on dialysis over five years. A further 180,000 people have been diagnosed with kidney disease.

Until recently, the course of kidney disease has been relentless and irreversible. But thanks to new treatments, if the disease is detected early, in many cases it can be slowed dramatically.

Bhupinder Manz, who averted kidney disease for 20 years by taking a test, with daughters Halina and Jatiner

fortunate. It was just such a test that flagged up her kidney disease at an early stage. On the Pill, Manz developed high blood pressure. A test revealed high levels of protein in her urine and she was told, "One day your kidneys will fail".

"South Asians such as Manz and Afro-Caribbeans are three to five times more likely to develop kidney disease," says Dr Elizabeth Lightstone, honorary consultant physician at London's Hammersmith Hospital.

With careful monitoring of her blood pressure and medication, Manz was able to delay her condition for almost 20 years, during which she followed a career as a local government officer, married and had two daughters. And Manz was doubly lucky. She was 37 when her kidneys failed, but after seven years on dialysis, she received a kidney transplant. Today she feels "almost normal" again.

cancerous kidney removed, yet despite her medical history her family GP merely prescribed anti-nausea pills.

Finally the little girl was rushed to the Royal Manchester Children's Hospital, where a tumour was diagnosed on the surviving kidney. Despite two operations, it could not be saved.

In February, Delise received a new kidney, perfectly matched, from a living donor—her mother Romina. "Delise has been incredibly brave," says Romina. "But if only she'd been given a urine test at the outset, she needn't have suffered for so long."

At the age of 18, Bhupinder Manz from Southall, London, was more

Condition Red

People with diabetes are hardest hit by kidney disease. Each year over 1,000 develop end-stage renal failure.

Another troublesome fact is the link between kidney disease and cardiac or circulatory problems. People

PHOTOGRAPHED BY NICK DAWE

who have diabetes or high blood pressure with excess protein in their urine have a far greater risk of suffering a heart attack or stroke. "Early screening of patients with diabetes is vital," says Anthony Barnett, professor of Medicine and head of Diabetes Science at Birmingham Heartlands and Solihull Hospital.

The good news, says Barnett, is that new blood-pressure drugs called angiotensin II receptor blockers even reduce pressure inside the kidneys. Studies show these drugs have cut organ-damage rates by 70 per cent. With their aid, a third of those diagnosed with early kidney disease have regained normal kidney function.

Five years after being diagnosed with Type 2 diabetes, John Gaffney's regular urine test showed up protein. Gaffney, a retired clerical worker from Solihull, had kidney disease and high blood pressure. But thanks to drug treatment, his kidney function is restored to such a degree that he should lead a relatively normal life for years.

Twenty-five years ago, Professor Feehally points out, few people knew the importance of checking cholesterol levels as pointers for cardiovascular disease. That's where we are today with kidney disease and levels of protein in urine. He and others urge anyone at high risk to ask for a urine test when they see their doctor. Or consumers can self-test at home.

It may even save your life.

This month, Reader's Digest readers can buy The National Kidney Research Fund's kidney test kit (produced by Wellbeing MET), for £4.50 including p&p. (Normal price is £5.50.)

Call the NKRF's helpline on 0845 300149, quoting reference RD99, or e-mail helpline@nkrf.org.uk.

INSIDE STORY

Most of the time, says a woman whose job combines office work with outside assignments, she is eager to get out. But when she glanced out of the window after the year's first snowstorm and saw the cars struggling through the frozen streets, she remarked, "Now starts the winter of my desk content."

"ALMANAC" in Minneapolis Tribune

WARM WELCOME?

Outside our local corner shop in Edinburgh, John the shopkeeper was sprinkling salt on the pavement to combat the freezing conditions. He saw my mother approaching and wished her "Seasonings greetings".

DAVID BANKS, Edinburgh

RD European of the Year
Peter Eigen

Dreaming of an Honest World

Angered by corruption in governments everywhere, Peter Eigen set up a team to fight it | BY BRIAN EADS

FROM A CRAGGY ESCARPMENT high above Kenya's Turkwel River, the middle-aged lawyer peered down a narrow, 150-metre-deep canyon. Government officials wanted to build a hydroelectric dam across the gorge. Peter Eigen, however, wondered if the project was really necessary. And so the World Bank's director for East Africa went to find out.

On horseback, he explored the forbidding landscape. Tribesman told him they needed the jobs construction would bring. But many people believed the dam would be inefficient. Worse, Eigen learned that damming the river would destroy forests, endangering the livelihood of nomadic herdsmen. Every expert he questioned was against the multi-million-pound dam, except Kenyan ministers and French diplomats.

Nonetheless, the dam was built, with expensive loans from France. As predicted, forests began to die and nomads drifted into urban slums. Eigen was disgusted, convinced that "the project was driven by corruption".

There were other dubious schemes. Officials in Mombasa rejected a £15- to £25-million repair plan for the city's broken water mains, yet approved a project costing about £170 million. A new four-lane motorway was built through the Rift Valley that few people used; a busy existing road could have been repaired for a fraction of the cost.

As a World Bank official, Eigen had encountered cases of corruption before. In Kenya, he realised that fraud and graft were routine and systemic, flourishing in the dark, opaque world of government contracting.

When he appealed to his bosses to confront the issue head-on they refused. When he spoke out they told him to stop. Corruption was taboo, one bank veteran told Reader's Digest.

FRUSTRATED AND DISILLUSIONED, Eigen quit the bank in 1991 and departed Kenya under a cloud. "I left like a betrayed lover," he says. At the age of 53 and entitled to a full pension, some men would have retreated into embittered retirement. Not Peter Eigen.

"I was determined to show them I would not give up without a fight."

He went on to create Transparency International (TI), a non-governmental organisation active in some 80 countries. Thanks to TI, corruption is now on almost everyone's agenda. After years of effort, anti-corruption laws exist where they never did—and principles of transparency, accountability and public scrutiny are acknowledged almost universally as essentials of good governance. To celebrate TI's achievements, Reader's Digest names Peter Eigen our 2004 European of the Year.

A NATIVE OF Augsburg in southern Germany, Peter Eigen studied at the University of Kansas. Then he took four months travelling in Latin America, working his passage home from Argentina as a deckhand. "Latin America was an important continent for me," Eigen says. "I became sensitive to injustice."

After earning a PhD at Frankfurt and passing the Bar exam in Munich, Eigen became a lawyer at World Bank headquarters in Washington DC. He rose through the ranks until his experiences in Kenya told him he could do more good for the developing world on the outside.

Eigen soon realised that fighting global corruption in his spare time was unrealistic, so he began building a network of supporters. German aid agency GTZ and the Global Coalition for Africa pledged cash and offered their help.

TI was launched in May 1993.

"Companies do not want to bribe," Eigen says. "They only bribe because their competitors do." His idea was to get them publicly to agree not to.

Eigen showed in Ecuador how it could work. That country was no stranger to corruption; in one episode officials are believed to have squandered several million pounds in a murky deal for railway engines, which ended up rusting in storage because they were too heavy for local tracks.

In the autumn of 1993, however, all bidders for a petroleum refinery project were forced to sign an "integrity pact". The process of choosing a contractor was conducted openly and went through without sweeteners.

TI HAD WON a landmark victory, and as news spread Eigen was deluged with calls, from Russia to Zaire, Mexico to Nepal, by people wanting to join his campaign. He badgered Berlin's Technical University into giving him a room, rent free, started recruiting volunteers and hired TI's first paid employee Margit Van Ham.

Eigen himself took no wages. In fact, TI had so little money, Van Ham says, that it waited until the third warning before paying phone and fax bills.

Peter Eigen: "I would not give up without a fight"

Sometimes the lines were disconnected. "Peter's stubbornness was crucial," she says. "When people laughed at him or despised him, he kept going."

Eigen and his colleagues identified 50 anti-corruption principles for use by national branches and local groups. In time, his three handwritten pages were expanded into a 364-page manual on building good governance, accountability and a system of national integrity.

Still, Eigen's former employer resisted. "The World Bank's legal department persistently sabotaged our efforts," he says.

Instead he took his case to the Organisation for Economic Co-operation and Development (OECD) in Paris, the 30-member group of rich countries committed to good governance and free trade. In most of them, paying bribes abroad was not illegal.

Eigen told OECD bosses that criminalising bribery was essential. Thanks in part to his resolve, the OECD has condemned bribery and by last year every OECD member country had passed new domestic laws against it.

TI's BRANCHES and volunteers have time and again shown that corruption is not just about multi-million-pound business deals. In Bangladesh, for example, teachers extort payment to put a child in school. Gas meter readers get bribes not to inflate the bill; bureaucrats, judges, clerks and policemen demand money to produce a document or schedule a hearing.

For businessmen in Bangladesh, getting the right paperwork for an export order can entail under-the-table payments to 50 people. Even medical staff get bribed to treat patients.

When TI reported such scams, it was front page news. Manzoor Hasan, the barrister heading the national branch, received death threats.

But many of Bangladesh's younger politicians have pledged support for TI's goals. Committees of "concerned citizens" have sprung up and the government promises an independent anti-corruption commission.

Still, last year Bangladesh remained the worst performer on the "corruptions perception index"—133rd of 133 countries. (The least corrupt nation was Finland. Russian and Chinese businesses were deemed most likely to offer and pay bribes.) Nobody, certainly not Peter Eigen, suggests that tackling deep-rooted corruption is easy.

EIGEN HAS UPSET many people along the way: those who profit from corruption, businessmen, development professionals, even collaborators who disagree with his more robust methods.

Yet, he has also made friends and allies beyond his expectations. Even China, notoriously corrupt and with no tradition of "civil society", has enlisted TI's help in setting up an anti-corruption school at the University of Hunan, Changsha. The four-year course will train cadres for the ruling Communist Party's Inspection and Discipline Commission.

A T AGE 65, Eigen will be stepping down soon from his post as executive chairman of TI. He knows his efforts have only scratched the surface. But he is optimistic. "We may sometimes be used as a fig leaf," he says. "We have to make sure it is a transparent fig leaf! If only ten per cent of people take this seriously, this is a tremendous gain."

Evidence of his progress came last April when he returned to Kenya. There, he was fêted by newly elected President Mwai Kibaki, who affirmed his commitment to eradicating corruption and has since launched a massive anti-corruption drive. Joining in the celebration was James Wolfensohn, president of the World Bank.

"It was a closing of the circle," Eigen says. "I felt vindicated."

THORN IN YOUR SIDE

I asked my friend how she was coping with her injured foot.

"It's a pain in the neck," she replied.

MALCOLM ELLIS, Chilwell, Nottinghamshire

READER'S DIGEST

ALL NEW!
BIGGER, BRIGHTER MAPS

The Complete Driver's Atlas of Britain & Ireland

THE ONLY ROAD ATLAS YOU'LL EVER NEED!

ONLY
£29.99

Ask for this book on a 7 day home trial...

simply call our hotline FREE on **0800 11 55 55** quoting reference no. 149-0

In the brand-new The Complete Driver's Atlas of Britain & Ireland from Reader's Digest:

- **568 pages**
- **Size 290mm x 230mm (11$^{7}/_{16}$" x 9$^{1}/_{16}$")**
- **Hard-wearing cover**
- **Sturdy, flexible plastic case to keep guide in perfect condition**
- **High-quality production means each colour stands out for unsurpassed clarity**
- **19 pages of congestion maps**
- **102 pages of town plans**
- **88 pages of touring information**
- **Over 200 colour photographs and illustrations**
- **Full index of nearly 30,000 placenames**
- **Ribbon marker to find your page quickly**

When You're Too Shy

Heart racing?
Hands shaking?
Help is here

BY JOANNIE SCHROF AND
STACEY SCHULTZ

IT IS SOMETHING of a miracle that Grace, a 35-year-old, is sitting in a cafe in town simply having lunch. Her careful, tiny bites of a sandwich may seem unremarkable, but for her they are an accomplishment. During her school years she was unable to eat in the dining hall, because she imagined her classmates' eyes boring into her. Only in her twenties, when panic attacks began to hit, did she learn she had a condition called social anxiety disorder, also known as social

ILLUSTRATED BY PAUL BLOW

phobia. Despite some success with therapy and medication, Grace still struggles. "I would be a different person in a different place if I didn't have to deal with this on a daily basis," she says.

Shyness is an almost universal human trait. Virtually everyone has bouts of it, and half of college students in a survey described themselves as shy. But studies show that at some point in their lives, one in eight people becomes so timid that they suffer from social phobia. During certain kinds of encounters, the heart races, palms sweat, the mouth goes dry, words vanish, thoughts become cluttered and an urge to escape takes over.

Some sufferers refuse to eat out or talk on the phone. Others go mute in front of their boss or a member of the opposite sex. At the extreme, they build a hermitic life, avoiding virtually all contact with others.

Getting Worse? Though social anxiety's symptoms have been noted since Hippocrates' time, the disorder didn't make its way into psychiatric manuals until 1980.

Certain people are born with a tendency towards extreme shyness—though biology is by no means destiny. Jerome Kagan, a researcher from Harvard University, has shown that by 16 weeks of age, babies display a predisposition towards shyness or boldness. Roughly one in five will thrash or cry when stimulated by something new, while others reach out to touch strangers or grab new objects.

Yet some shy babies may become gregarious children and outgoing infants may become shy, even socially phobic, adults.

Life experiences can mould the brain to become more or less shy over time. Psychologists note that the brain appears to attach a fear marker to the details (place, time of day, background music, etc) of a traumatic situation. So, for example, when a child gets told off by a teacher, the pupil will feel nervous the next few times he or she steps into that classroom. But sometimes the brain is too good at making those associations and the anxiety is triggered by any classroom or teacher.

The classic behaviour of children who do not know how to handle these "daggers to the heart", says psychiatrist Moira Rynn, is to avoid any attention at all. They may stop inviting friends over, speak only to certain people or refuse to go to school. By avoiding the very situations they need to be in to learn social skills, these children diminish their ability to cope.

Parent's Message A highly critical parent can train a child to cower—but even the gentlest parent can bring up a fearful child. "If parents avoid social situations or worry excessively about what the neighbours think", explains Richard Heimberg, director of an adult anxiety clinic in Philadelphia, "the message to a child is that the world is full of danger and humiliation."

Social phobia affects about half its victims by the age of eight and many others during adolescence. Some live with an undetected problem that surfaces when facing a new public arena, such as university or a new job. More women than men are thought to suffer from social anxiety, but because shyness is less acceptable in males, more men seek help.

Social phobia hit Steve Fox so hard in secondary school that girls made a sport of saying hello just to watch him turn bright red. He refused to speak in class and never asked a girl out; even walking in front of people left him with sweaty palms.

By the time he was 19, his father was concerned enough to find a doctor, and a combination of medication and therapy helped him recover. Now 27, Fox has given a speech in front of 1,700 people—and he married one of the girls at school who used to tease him.

When the socially anxious turn to professionals for help, they usually start with a few months of cognitive behavioural therapy. The idea is to fight what psychiatrist Isaac Tylim calls the intellectual core of social phobia: the belief that others will judge you negatively and humiliation will result. "I turn down invitations to go to lunch with people I admire, even though I desperately want to go," says one woman. "I assume that when we get together, they'll regret having asked and want to get away from me."

Spectrum of Shyness

Normal Shyness

- Jittery starting a speech, but later glad you did it.
- Mind goes blank on first date, but eventually you're able to talk.
- Palms sweat in a job interview, but you answer questions thoughtfully.

Extreme Shyness

- Heart races when you know people are looking at you.
- Tremble when speaking at a meeting, even if only saying your name.
- Avoid starting a conversation for fear of saying something awkward.

Social Phobia

- Do anything to avoid being introduced to new people.
- Have trouble swallowing in public, making it hard to dine out.
- Feel you never make a good impression; believe you're a social failure.

Severe Social Phobia

- Calm only when alone; can barely leave the house.
- Constantly worry others will embarrass or humiliate you.
- Have frequent panic attacks; leave room rather than converse.

Through therapy, phobics learn to replace faulty thoughts with realistic ones and to question the fears that paralyse them.

Perhaps the most salient feature of social anxiety is the sensation of being so overwhelmed that panic sets in. Almost everyone occasionally feels this during the first minute or so of a speech, for instance. For most, the discomfort soon subsides. But a social phobic can suffer for more than an hour, with the anxiety subsiding only because of exhaustion. Behavioural therapists often coach social phobics to remain in terrifying situations until the symptoms abate and it is clear that nothing bad is going to happen.

Meeting Strangers

The first place Melinda Stanley, a US professor of psychiatry and behavioural therapy, takes many patients is an auditorium. Standing in front of a small audience, the patient practises giving a brief talk. "Sometimes it takes a long time," Stanley says, "but the phobic's heart will eventually stop racing for fear of what the audience might think of him."

Other therapists take phobics on practice runs of situations that are embarrassing to them, like walking through a crowded hotel lobby.

Because some social phobics are out of the habit of talking to others, therapists help them brush up on social skills. For example, it never dawns on many of the most shy that they should say hello to a person in a social situation. And they are often stuck in the conversation-killing habit of answering questions with one-word responses.

Party Phobia?

Dreading that New Year's Eve party? You're not alone. Here are five tips to help you cope, from consultant clinical psychologist Professor Adrian Wells, patron of the National Phobics Society:

- *Don't think about the party beforehand*
- *Go with a friend*
- *Focus on others, not yourself*

Concentrate your attention on what's going on around you, on people's clothes, the decor, rather than how *you're* coming across. You'll feel less nervous.

- *Slip into a small group* Smile, then just listen for a minute to the free-floating conversation. It will help you think of things to say.
- *Talk to someone* Offer a compliment, such as "I really like your tie", or ask a question. Most people are flattered by attention and warm to someone eager to listen.

"I learned that if someone doesn't seem interested in the first sentence out of my mouth, I shouldn't just walk away," says Rick Robbins, 35, whose social anxiety contributed to his dropping out of college. "Now, before I go out, I come up with four or five topics to talk about. Usually I find something in common and forget my nerves."

Bernardo Carducci, director of The Shyness Research Institute at Indiana University, is convinced that shifting the focus away from the self is the most therapeutic thing a shy person can do. He sends patients to soup kitchens, hospitals and nursing homes to escape the tyranny of self-centredness. "It works because you see how shy other people can be," says Robbins. "And then you don't feel so alone, so different from everyone else."

In severe cases drugs can help, although the perfect medication has yet to be found. Most popular now are the antidepressants known as SSRIs (selective serotonin reuptake inhibitors), such as Paroxetine, which is branded as Seroxat.

Lynne Henderson, director of a shyness clinic in California, worries that drugs are often used as temporary crutches. "People tend to relapse when they get off the medication," she warns. Research indicates that over time, therapy might serve a person better.

Therapists say that if the socially phobic could rein in their anxiety enough to function, they would help make the world a better place. Many famous celebrities like Woody Allen and Sir Michael Caine have suffered from shyness, as have well-loved figures in history, such as Albert Einstein and Charlotte Brontë. Shyness in its milder forms is associated with empathy, perceptiveness, intuition and sensitivity—all qualities that are nothing to be shy about.

_____

Have you ever suffered from shyness or social anxiety? Write to the address on page 10 or e-mail YouSaidIt@readersdigest.co.uk.

For information on social phobia and details about therapies, call the National Phobics Society on 0870 770 0456 or go to www.readersdigest.co.uk.

COURTING TROUBLE

Being under oath does not absolve one from saying something stupid, as these actual transcripts prove:

Q: Officer, when you stopped the defendant, was your blue light flashing?
A: Yes.

Q: Did the defendant say anything when she got out of her car?
A: Yes.
Q: What did she say?
A: "What disco am I at?"

Q: Do you recall the time that you examined the body?
A: The post-mortem started around 8.30pm.
Q: And Mr Dennington was dead at the time?
A: No, he was sitting on the table wondering why I was doing a post-mortem on him.

Journal of Court Reporting Online

British student Matthew Scott tells of his escape from kidnappers last September and his 12-day survival ordeal

Lost
in the
Jungle

BY MATTHEW SCOTT
AS TOLD TO PETER FOSTER AND CAROLINE DAVIES

'Sorry, señor,' said the guy at the seafront tourist agency in Santa Marta, Colombia, 'the tour left half an hour ago.' Oh no—I'd done it again! I was famous for failing to make my connections. I'd even managed to miss the plane taking me to South America at the start of my gap-year travels. Now, after seven months away, I was looking forward to returning to my family in London and taking up my engineering place at university. But before I left I had one more adventure planned, a six-day trek into the jungle to visit the remains of the Lost City. It was going to be the perfect end to my trip—except that I'd just missed it.

BUT I WASN'T GOING TO GIVE UP just yet. I tore through the streets back to my £3-a-night hostel, determined to catch up with the tour by nightfall. Hastily stuffing a pair of black Wellingtons, a water bottle and a smelly old T-shirt into a dilapidated rucksack, I raced for a bus which would take me towards base camp.

In my mind the Lost City, dating from 500 BC but only discovered in 1976, was a must-see. Even though there were several terrorist groups operating in the area, I didn't think I was doing anything risky. I had talked to many other travellers who had been there.

The bus stopped in a small Indian village and a local guide agreed to take me up to the camp. As we climbed the steep path I was struck by the beauty of the mountains. Their sharp slopes were clad in thick jungles and criss-crossed with rivers and streams. My guide told me that the largest river, the Buritaca, was the main route up to the Lost City.

At the camp I was relieved to meet up with the others in our group. I was the youngest, the rest were all in their mid-twenties or older: Mathijs, a good chess player from Holland; Reinhilt, a German girl keen on mountaineering; and half a dozen Israelis. They told me there was another group of trekkers at a nearby camp that we might join up with.

That morning I'd been talking to an ice-cream seller about visiting the Lost City. He told me it wasn't worth the hassle. But that first night, when we trooped off to swim in a river with a waterfall, I knew he was wrong.

I stood above the rock pool, looking out over the jungle—feeling the karma—then jumped. For a second I hung in the air, then—whoooosh—I plunged into the freezing water. It was so cold. But I felt pretty good. Things were finally going to plan. I had caught up with the tour, I was going to complete this last trip and then I was going home. Life was sweet.

Capture

"Get up." The words were in Spanish. Then came a prod in the ribs with the butt of a rifle, not hard but insistent. The voice spoke louder. "Get up! Get up!" What was going on?

I could see two men in uniform, with camouflage caps, black flak jackets and holsters with pistols. Each had a larger gun across his chest and they were searching our bags. I glanced at my watch, a cheap digital. 5.09am.

Suddenly I was on my feet and alert. I had my clothes on in two seconds flat. My first thought was, "This is a robbery." Then I saw them tying up the guide and the porter, who weren't protesting.

Despite this, everyone stayed calm. It was surreal. We'd all got to know each other over the past two days, hiking along the river, falling asleep to the sound of crickets and frogs and rushing water—"God's symphony" someone had called it. We'd bonded. And now we were being kidnapped.

We were herded into the middle of the room and the intruders demanded our nationalities. I snatched a word with the tour guide, since I'd acquired passable Spanish. I figured he ought to know the local paramilitary groups.

"Is this a problem?"

"Ningún problema." No problem.

He was lying, of course, but it made me feel better. I picked

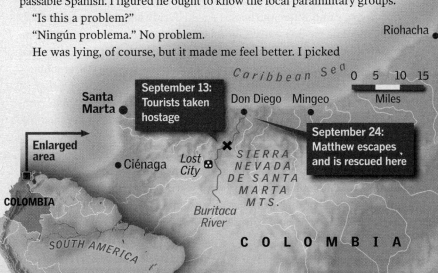

up my bag and the two armed men marched us all down the hill to the other tourist camp. I wondered if I could keep going, straight out of the Lost City, and find my way back the way we had come. But when we reached the second camp there were 16 or 17 more men standing around with machine guns. At this point I realised I might be in trouble.

Now or Never

Among the second group was another Briton, Mark Henderson, a 31-year-old TV producer I'd met the night before. We had a lot in common since we both came from the same area of south London. Now, as the guerrillas split us into two groups, I made sure I was with Mark.

There were eight of us in all, including Reinhilt, a Spaniard with a thick Basque-country accent, and four Israelis. We were told to fill our water bottles and then, accompanied by eight armed guards, we were given the order to march. It was now 5.30am.

Our direction led deep into the jungle, away from the Lost City. A guerrilla led the way, with another bringing up the rear; the rest mingled with the column which soon dissolved into a straggle.

The jungle was thick and lush and we had to grab on to vines to avoid slipping on the muddy paths. I caught up with the lead guerrilla to try and make conversation. At first he said the guerrillas were Colombian army taking us away from bandits, and then that they would be returning to Santa Marta the next day. Finally, he admitted that we were on a two-day march to a camp where the bosses would decide what to do with us.

By the time we had walked for four hours everyone was tired. The sun was beating down on the jungle canopy, generating the heat and vapour that would soon turn into the rain that fell like clockwork every afternoon.

Finally, the guerrillas called a halt and we were each given a slice of processed cheese and some panella—a honey derivative that comes compacted into a thick disc, with bees entombed inside. It's pretty inedible, but I tried to take as much as possible as it was passed around, breaking up little bits to put in my water bottle. At least it might give me energy.

After we had eaten, the march began again. Soon, we breached the tree-line, moving through a scrubby landscape with rocks jutting out of the side of the mountain. Some of the weaker members were starting to feel the pace. I heard a couple of the Israelis behind me complaining to the guards.

"We don't want to go any further. Where are you taking us anyway?"

I couldn't hear what the guards said in reply, but when I turned back

one of them pointed his gun at me. The message was clear: get walking.

Apart from this, there was no trouble with our captors. They didn't push or kick us. We'd spent the past two days walking through the mountains with guides and this wasn't much different. Except now the guides had guns.

Shortly after midday we stopped for a second time as it began to rain. Each of us was issued with a sheet of plastic to keep out the wet. There were also meagre rations, a mini chocolate bar and bits of guava solid.

The guards were scrupulous in picking up the chocolate wrappings and people commented on it.

"How nice they don't want to litter the mountainside."

But Mark and I realised it wasn't that at all—it was because they didn't want our group to be tracked. As we trudged higher and higher into the mountains, we discussed our predicament. We didn't talk about "escaping" because the Spanish word—escapar—is too similar. Instead, we said we were thinking of "getting away".

There were two possibilities. First, to hide in the jungle until the column had passed by, then retrace the route to the Lost City and Santa Marta. There was the risk, however, of meeting more guerrillas on the way. The second option was to follow a stream down the mountain until it connected with the Río Buritaca, which would lead us back to Santa Marta.

"Let's go now," I said.

"I think it's a bad idea."

"Come on, we can do it. We're in better shape than the others."

Mark shook his head. "Too risky."

Clearly there were risks—getting lost, or being caught and shot. But I was pretty confident we wouldn't be shot. Hostages are more valuable alive than dead and the guerrillas seemed pretty demoralised.

It was now 1pm and soon the rain would be so strong that we would have to stop. The window of opportunity was closing.

As we strode on I was boiling with fury. I couldn't stand the thought of months in the jungle while my life was put on hold. My flight to England was in five days' time. I had planned on going home to my family and then to university. I didn't want these people to ruin all that.

I made up my mind—I'd follow the river system back to Santa Marta. After alerting Mark and the others, I found a spot in the line where I could not be seen by our captors. I could hear the water on my right-hand side.

I couldn't wait any longer.

Alone

I launched myself feet first off the right-hand side of the narrow ridge, the thick layer of cloud and driving rain helping conceal my departure. I thought it might be half an hour before I was missed.

Despite this, as I slid on my backside down the steep slope, I was scared I might have been spotted and followed. I scrambled urgently down the scree of rocks and loose tree roots, razor-sharp twigs lacerating my bare arms and my feet skidding in my Wellington boots. Eventually I came to a halt. It was time to take stock.

I took off my rucksack and calculated which of the things inside I needed. The sack had holes in it—I'd spent ages trying to sew them up—and even though it left my arms free, it inhibited my full range of movement. So I decided to leave it behind. I also threw away my water bottle; since my plan was to follow the river, I reckoned I'd have a regular supply of drinking water.

I decided to keep a torch, the spare sock which contained my cash card and the plastic sheet, which was essential—my only shelter against the rain and cold. I rolled it up and stuffed it into one of my Wellingtons. I put the sock in the other boot and the torch into my trouser pocket. That left just the clothes I was wearing: a T-shirt, trousers, swimming trunks and socks.

I moved on quickly, still thinking that I might be being pursued. Suddenly, one foot gave way and I found myself falling, tumbling over and over, grabbing wildly at vines and roots as I tried to steady myself. I must have dropped more than 40 feet.

"There's no way they're following me down that," I said out loud, sure that I was now safe from the guerrillas. Thankful I hadn't broken any bones, I carried on. The descent was now dangerously steep. I turned to face the rock and began to climb down, looking for hand- and footholds. It wasn't easy in Wellingtons, but the vines on the trees were generally good. Then

SUDDENLY I FOUND MYSELF FALLING, tumbling over and over, grabbing wildly at vines. I must have dropped more than 40 feet

one of them broke and I fell, hitting my jaw on a ledge of rock. It bled a lot.

I carried on for two hours and, when it got dark, I lay down on the slope, curled up in the plastic sheet. But I couldn't sleep. It was too wet and cold and my mind was racing. *How was I going to survive out here in the jungle? How long would it take to find my way back along the river to Santa Marta?*

In the morning I located the stream that I had heard from up on the ridge. Here my Wellington boots came into their own. The fastest way through the jungle was to walk along the bed of the stream, but even that was overgrown with plants. Sometimes I ended up on all fours, crawling along the stream to get under fallen trees that blocked the way. I regularly ran into steep waterfalls and was forced to decide the best way to go. Should I head into the jungle to find an easier descent? Or clamber down the wet rocks?

The cold and the wet were my main enemies, in a valley so deep that the sun's warmth couldn't penetrate. My theory was that the stream would soon bend to the right to join up with the Río Buritaca, which would lead me back to the coast.

I tried to think positively. I'd make it back in a couple of days, I reckoned. I was 100 per cent certain I was going to be all right.

'Tomorrow I'll Find the River'

That first day I established a routine that I followed for four days. Rising at 5.30am—my watch kept me sane—I walked hard until eight, then climbed up the valley slope to find some sun. I allowed myself an hour's rest to warm up, then plunged back down into the gloom of the valley.

As I scrambled along the stream I sang songs, mostly desolate ones about being lost, forcing myself to keep pace with the rhythm of the tune. Though I hadn't eaten anything I didn't feel hungry. You get hungry when there's food available and here there was no food at all. There were no berries, no fruit, no wildlife but for birds, which I couldn't catch.

The only creatures available were bugs. The masses of mosquitoes drove me crazy, though fortunately this part of Colombia was not malarial. After a while, I learned to cope with them by playing a game—seeing how long I could resist swatting them. Another bigger insect bit even harder. Whenever one of these bloodsuckers landed on me, I would catch it and squeeze its juices on to my tongue—it had a sweet taste I shall never forget.

Later, I pulled the scab off the cut on my chin and ate it. I reasoned it must have some nutritional value.

At 2pm every day the rains came—bruising, torrential, unforgiving. It was impossible to walk any more, so I went to bed, curled under my plastic sheet. I lay in a foetal position, trying to make a cocoon of warmth, but it was as wet inside as out. By the time the rain stopped, if it did, it was pitch-dark.

My jungle nights lasted for some 15 hours. I'd just lie there, trying to sleep, listening to the whining of the mosquitoes, croaking of the frogs and incessant rush of water. Sometimes I thought those nights would never end.

Lost

On the fifth day, I couldn't fool myself any longer. I knew I should be heading north, yet had worked out from the sun's position that the stream was taking me south-west—deeper into the jungle. It was clear I wasn't going to find the Río Buritaca that day or any other. I was in the wrong

river system and hopelessly lost.

Matthew's gear, including a plastic sheet, "my shelter against the rain and cold"

The next day was my lowest point. At this stage I really regretted escaping and would have gone back to my captors with open arms. I hadn't seen any sign of life at all for nearly a week—I was probably in a place where no humans had ever been before. Another week like this and I would certainly be dead. I put my chances of survival now at 50–50.

Though there didn't seem much hope, I just kept pressing on. I thought of my family and friends back in London and all the plans I had made, like going to university. I really didn't want to miss the start of term, but all of that seemed to exist in a different world.

To keep me going I also made resolutions. If I ever got out of this, I promised to appreciate every second of my life. I swore I'd remember that each meal is a luxury that many can ill afford. And I promised myself that I would be more open and honest with everyone, especially my family.

Survival

I was finding it impossible to sleep for more than an hour a night. And now the cold and lack of food was starting to make me hallucinate. Once, I imagined I could go to the shop on the corner and rent a horse to get out of the jungle. Why on earth hadn't I thought of it before?

Boredom led me to fantasise and I craved food and warmth. I imagined walking into a restaurant and ordering soup, perhaps tomato. And I wanted a baked potato, cut into quarters, with a little butter and a lot of salt, and then a huge amount of cheese. That was very important. You couldn't put too much cheese on and it had to be cheddar. And, on top of that, chutney. Not pickle, chutney.

I fantasised about food every night. "When I get home," I said to myself, "I'll learn to cook."

I tried not to look at my watch as that made the time go even more slowly.

Up on the Ridge

I decided to abandon the stream and make for the ridge. On day seven I started at 5.30, as usual, but I felt light-headed and weak—the climbing was taking its toll. Then, miraculously, I stumbled across a path cutting across the valley; there was a camp, or some kind of construction, at the bottom. It was an absolute miracle. Though I'm an atheist, I sank to my knees and gave thanks to God. I didn't know what else to do.

The camp consisted of a little platform with four poles for a mosquito net and, on a fifth pole, an empty plastic packet of peas and carrots. I felt so happy. It was the first trace I had seen of humanity.

But as the path led upwards again, I could only manage about ten paces before I had to sit down and rest. I only made it about halfway up the hill before the two o'clock deluge.

That "night" was the worst so far. As well as being on a steep slope, which gave me bad pressure sores, there was a tropical storm with lightning and thunder which just rolled on and on. The rain was bruising. Every time I changed position, the plastic and I slithered down the slope.

As I was no longer close to the river, I had no drinking water. I had been using the front section of my torch as a cup. Though it leaked around the lens, I could get a decent mouthful from the river if I used it quickly enough.

But the torch end wasn't much use now. I had to come up with a plan to catch some of the water cascading down all around me. I took off my boots and set them down with sticks in the top to hold them open. But when I next slithered down the slope, I knocked the boots over. After that, I placed them above my position and, to my relief, they did trap some rain.

Now I was higher up, there was a view. The next day, I heard a wonderful, man-made sound. The throb of distant helicopters. Suddenly one was coming towards me. It was overhead, 160 feet away. Surely they were looking for me. I waved and jumped up and down and threw my plastic sheet in the air. They didn't see me. The sound died away.

Sick

By the tenth day, I was feeling sick, dizzy and nauseous, collapsing frequently as I pressed uphill. My feet were painful and clearly infected. I was worried I had trench foot, which is caused by water, and I was still using my Wellingtons to catch the rain at night. But I had to drink and, during the day, regularly sucked moisture from the spare sock in my boot.

I arrived on a ridge above a wide, flat valley. I could see irregular green shapes carved out of the jungle below that looked like signs of human activity. My heart leapt. If the land was cultivated, that meant permanent residents, almost certainly Indians.

I found an abandoned hut, containing pots, a water bottle and a gourd. There were also some rotten potatoes—the first food I'd seen. I was tempted

Letting them go was probably the worst decision of my life. I thought to myself

'WHAT AN ABSOLUTE FOOL I AM'

to eat them though in the end I decided not to. I knew that if left too long, potatoes turn green and create a toxin—they wouldn't do me any good.

"I'll find people tomorrow," I told myself.

I had to.

Welcome Encounter

The next morning I rounded a corner and stopped in amazement. Ahead of me on the path were two donkeys who quickly shied off when I approached. Then I saw five cows beside a path leading to two large houses surrounded by a fence of thick vegetation.

"Hola!" I shouted, however there was no reply. The houses were abandoned. I was keeping a tight rein on my emotions yet I really had hoped there would be somebody.

I thought back on my life, on what an easy 19 years it had been. To think that I could just walk down the street and buy Coca-Cola. That I had spent every night of my life in a bed. That I used to eat good food, cuts of meat with rice and vegetables. Yet here I was, face to face with the effort it took for simple people to get food off the land.

These were my thoughts when, suddenly, I saw three figures walking towards me. They were Indians: a man, a woman and a girl. I was so happy.

They were absolutely astonished to see me. Fortunately they spoke a little Spanish.

"Hello. I haven't had food in 11 days. I have been lost." I tried to explain I'd been captured and had escaped.

I offered them money to guide me to Santa Marta. They said it would take three days. They gave me panella which I ate eagerly and drank a lot of their water. Then they told me to wait while they collected their donkeys.

After they'd gone, as I lay in the sun, I had terrible misgivings. I should never have let the Indians out of my sight. These were the first human beings I had seen in 11 days and I had just let them walk away. Now I had no idea if I would ever see them again.

"I'm a fool," I said. "An absolute fool." Letting them go might be the worst decision I had ever made in my life.

Rescue

To my relief, the Indians came back. We set off at once for their village, walking hard, and I struggled to keep up. I kept asking, "Are we nearly there yet?" Over and over like a child. Unlike the paramilitaries, who always said the next stop was "one hour" off, the Indians were cruelly honest. The village was still miles away.

As the rain began to fall, it became obvious that I wasn't going to make it that far. When we reached two huts occupied by an Indian woman called Oonca and her children, they finally agreed to call a halt.

Oonca took me into a hut with a fire. It was glorious. For the first time in 12 days, I began to dry out. I collapsed on to a hammock and they gave me two oranges, my first solid food. Then, as the others stoked the fire, I fell into a dreamless sleep.

Final Effort

ABBIE TRAYLER-SMITH

"We cheered when we saw him, but I was in tears," says Kate Scott, with Matthew and his father James

"Go! Go! Go!" The command was barely audible above the clatter of the rotor blades. The Colombian army helicopter touched down and I was lifted aboard by two soldiers. The door was still open as the helicopter wheeled away over the jungle towards Santa Marta. That morning, after three more hours of relentless walking behind my Indian rescuers, I'd stumbled into the village of Don Diego. And now, after 12 days in the Sierra Nevada, my ordeal was over.

In the hospital at Santa Marta, I was handed a mobile phone.

My dad picked up the phone at home in Clapham and I said, "Hello, big man, how's it going?"

"It's Matt!" he shouted. I could hear Mum crying in the background. When she came on the line she asked me what I wanted when I got home. "A baked potato," I said, "with lots of cheese and chutney."

WORDS FROM THE HINTERLANDS

The question we posed in Word Power this month (page 27) asked for country or place names with "land" in them. How many did you think of? Sorry, but no points for Never-Never Land, Land of Nod or Land of 1,000 Dances.

Besides the examples in the question, our list contained: Badlands (of South Dakota), Baffin Island (and lots of other islands in Canada), Deutschland, England, Finland, Greenland, Holland, Iceland, Ireland, Jutland, Lapland, Lolland (Denmark), Netherlands, New Zealand, Poland, Queensland (Australia), Rhineland, Swaziland, Switzerland, Thailand, Vinland, Zeeland. Did we miss any?

Buy-lines

When it's drab and dreary outside, shake off those winter blues with these ideas. if you would like further information on the products listed please tick the Reader Reply Card. *Kate Garratt*

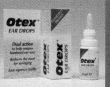

Improve your Health & Fitness

with the *Talking Pedometer*

Because Health & Comfort recognise the importance of exercise to health and well being, we are offering Reader's Digest subscribers an exclusive SALE PRICE OFFER on our best-selling Talking Pedometer.

This ingenious multi-function exercise aid works by measuring the distance you travel and the number of steps you take. Whether you walk, jog or run, it will record this information and tell you at the touch of a button!

Functions also include a digital time display with built-in alarm plus 7 built-in melodies that automatically increase or decrease in tempo as you change pace. The Talking Pedometer is so easy to use - just clip on to your waistband or belt and away you go!

ONLY £9.99!
PLUS P&P
RRP £29.99

BUY TWO SAVE OVER £5

"You have walked 1,245 steps. The distance is..."

- **The 'SELECT' button allows you to choose one of 7 melodies whilst you are exercising.**

- **Press the 'TALK' button and the Pedometer will tell you the time, the number of steps completed and the distance you have travelled.**

- **Clear digital display shows time, number of steps and distance travelled.**

FREE MYSTERY GIFT
Worth up to £9.99 with EVERY ORDER - while stocks last!
Order the Talking Pedometer within 14 days and claim your FREE Mystery Gift!

ORDER TODAY ON OUR HOTLINE 0870 054 66 55

Please quote code **TP012** Lines open: 8.30am to 9pm, 7 days a week. Customer Services Line: 0870 060 7

A Thank You They'll Remember

Who says good manners are stuffy? Here are some novel but sound ways to say thank you, from model, actress and etiquette expert Karen Duffy:

• Send a photograph of the gift in use (modelling the jumper, smelling the roses, driving the Mercedes). A friend wrote to say that her newborn son liked the overalls I sent so much he cried. She enclosed a photo of the little boy in the overalls, screaming his head off.

• Try writing a short poem of gratitude. A rhyming dictionary can help here.

• If you're going to a dinner party, why just bring another bottle of wine? Instead, consider what your hosts might enjoy after their guests have gone, such as a video or DVD and popcorn for a post-party afternoon on the sofa.

• You must send a thank-you note of some sort, even if you loathe the gift. Don't lie and don't be too honest; simply express appreciation for the thoughtfulness.

• A true present is given without strings, so you can exchange it without feeling guilty. Passing it on as a gift to someone else is also acceptable—just be sure you don't get caught out.

PHOTOGRAPHED BY PIERRE DUFOUR

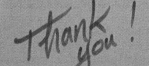

What's in a Cough?

SHOULD YOU see a doctor about that hack, or just wait for it to go away? Some pointers from GP and broadcaster Dr Mark Porter:

• Most winter coughs are caused by viral infection of the upper airways and go within three weeks. Coughs lasting longer are suspicious.

• All coughs accompanied by breathlessness should ring alarm bells—viral coughs do not generally cause this, so it could be a more serious infection, asthma or heart problems.

• Coughing up phlegm is part of normal recovery from a virus and in itself does not mean antibiotics are required. But blood-stained phlegm or yellow-green phlegm accompanied by a temperature warrant further investigation.

• Night-time coughing is suspicious. It's often a key feature of asthma or it may be a sign of heart failure.

• Babies and young children can be quite ill without an obviously troublesome cough. Their rate of breathing is a better measure: if your child has a cough and is breathing faster than normal, then they need to see a doctor.   Radio Times

Managing Migraines

ONE IN SIX Britons suffers migraines, yet 60% of them have never sought help. In fact there are many known triggers; if you keep a diary of where and when you have attacks you may establish which ones affect you. These are typical triggers (more at www.migrainetrust.org):

Stress or its removal (such as a holiday) or too little or too much sleep (weekend lie-in).

Foods Cheese, red wine or chocolate affect many; for others it's pickled, cured, smoked or fermented foods, or nuts, dairy, citrus fruits or caffeine.

Hormones The menstrual cycle is a factor for half of women sufferers.

Other Exercise, travel, skipping meals or even the weather may be a key.

The Healing Power of Hobbies

Gardening, stamp collecting, even competitive Scrabble, all keep us healthy—in both body and mind

AT LAST COUNT, Debbie Baker had 3,000 Barbie dolls. Her passion may seem odd, but experts agree that being an enthusiastic hobbyist is good for you.

Hobbies reduce stress, says Alice Domar, director of the Mind/Body Centre for Women's Health at Harvard Medical School. They distract you from everyday worries: if you're focused on the pottery you're making, you can't fret about work, says Domar. And knitting, or anything requiring repetitive motion, elicits the relaxation response, a feeling of overall serenity, marked by lowered blood pressure.

Hobbies provide a calming sense of control, says Domar, and research suggests this strengthens immunity. You may have little say at work, but when you're woodworking, you're in charge. You get the credit—and satisfaction—of a job well done.

We know that physical activity extends life, but less active pursuits are healthy as well. A Swedish study showed people who regularly engaged in hobbies such as sewing and gardening were less likely to suffer mental decline. Similar research published in *The New England Journal of Medicine* found those who pursued mind-boosting activities such as crossword puzzles lowered their risk of Alzheimer's or other dementia.

"Any hobby that challenges the brain should have a positive effect on dementia risk," says neurologist Joe Verghese, study co-author.

Many hobbies are social. From playing bridge to swapping tips with other collectors, engaging with like-minded souls boosts immunity. A Japanese study of almost 12,000 people found that men who engaged in hobbies or community activities were less likely to die of stroke or circulatory disorders than those who didn't.

So keep fishing or making model boats. Others may think your obsession is unhealthy—you know otherwise. **SHARI CAUDRON**

Pace Yourself

HERE'S A low-intensity slimming programme that might work for you. In the US the "America on the Move" scheme, developed by weight-loss experts, offers this challenge: take 2,000 extra steps a day to halt the one- to three-pound yearly weight gain that plagues most of us. Clip a pedometer to your waistband. Wear it for a week to find how many steps you take per day. Then up it by 2,000.

"Walking is a great way to exercise," says Susan Miller of British charity Weight Concern, "and pedometers are a fun way to do it." You can buy a pedometer for £13–18 from Boots or at www.gadgets.co.uk or www.dietandfitnessresources.co.uk.

IMAGE SUPPLIED BY WWW.UKGE.CO.UK

KILLING WITH KINDNESS

Pampering a suffering spouse may actually make them worse, say researchers from the University of Florida. They found that among men with chronic pain (mostly lower back pain), those with attentive wives

reported more pain. Female patients with attentive husbands didn't feel greater pain, but actually performed worse on physical tests such as walking and lifting. Study author Roger Fillingim theorises that by "rewarding" pain you may be effectively encouraging it.

Mums And Gums

IF YOU'RE expecting a baby, be diligent about dental hygiene: gum disease can increase the risk of premature birth, and a new study at the University of Alabama shows that the worse the infection, the worse the risk. But it also found that women with gum disease who got treatment before week 35 could cut their risk by as much as 84%. The British Dental Hygien-ists Association advises women considering pregnancy to have an oral examination.

PHOTOLIBRARY.COM

Could senna pills get any smaller?

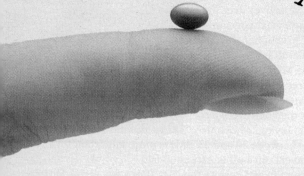

Made from **natural senna* extract**

For gentle, effective overnight relief of constipation

EX-LAX
SENNA PILLS (Sennosides)

PURIFIED SENNA EXTRACT

20 pills
SUGAR COATED

overnight relief

No odour, no taste, just natural senna* freedom packed into a tiny sugar-coated pill.

Natural senna micropills*

A gentle, predictable way to get that Ex-Lax feeling.

Always read the label. *Made from purified extract of natural senna. Contains Sennosides.

TLC for Your Liver

FEELING GUILTY about the punishment you meted out to your liver over the party season? Here's what you can do to make it up, says Christopher Day, Professor of Liver Medicine at the University of Newcastle Medical School:

- Have 2–3 alcohol-free days a week. It's better to have two or three drinks one night and none the next than one every day.
- Watch your weight! Try to keep your body mass index (BMI) between 20 and 25. BMI is more important for liver health than whether you eat olive oil or saturated fat.
- Milk thistle can help calm and cleanse the liver after a few nights partying.
- Keep your fluid-intake up—6–8 glasses a day. It doesn't have to be water.
- Eat a varied diet with plenty of antioxidants including vitamin E. Green vegetables, carrots and citrus fruits are all good sources.
- Keep your blood sugar level steady. Eat starchy foods rather than sugary snacks and limit alcohol consumption to meal times.

The fish is in the post

IF YOU'RE AFTER really fresh fish, have you thought about mail order? Several firms now despatch fish and seafood to UK addresses in insulated chiller boxes. The fish is likely to be fresher than you'd get from a fishmonger (you're just cutting out the middle man).

Fish Direct (0800 0272066) fish-direct.co.uk
Fowey Fish (01726 832422) foweyfish.com
Fresh Fish Online (0800 0857668)

fresh-fish-online.com
Island Seafare (01624 834494) www.islandseafare.co.uk
The Fish Society (0800 279 3474) www.thefishsociety.co.uk (frozen only but a wide choice of cuts)

DRINKING YOUR BONES AWAY?

New research suggests drinking a lot of cola could contribute to osteoporosis. Researchers at Tufts University, Massachusetts, found that women who drank more than three 340ml servings of cola a day had up to 5·1% lower bone mineral density than women who drank less than one. It may be that the phosphoric acid in cola binds with bone-friendly calcium in the gut and prevents it being absorbed. Men were unaffected.

Dear Esther

TV's **ESTHER RANTZEN** has been investigating **INJURY COMPENSATION** for people who have genuinely suffered after accidents which were not their fault. Here Esther helps people claim the compensation they deserve:

SHOULD I STILL CLAIM FOR MY ACCIDENT?

WHILST I WAS out shopping last year, I slipped and damaged my shoulder, which still causes me pain. I know it's a long time afterwards, but a friend says I could still claim compensation - is that true?

Colin, Shenley

◼ ESTHER SAYS:

I'm so sorry to hear your story. But the good news is that you are still entitled to make a personal injury claim up to 3 years after the accident happened.

My advice would be to call the Accident Advice Helpline now on 0800 0375 375 and you should be able to find out within 5 minutes if your claim can go ahead. Their specialist panel of solicitors will do all the work on your behalf on a NO WIN, NO FEE basis, so you have nothing to lose.

Esther Rantzen

Esther Rantzen

- ● **FREE expert advice**
- ● **FAST & simple process by phone**
- ● **Even the call is FREE**

THANKS!

THANK YOU

I picked up the phone and within minutes I discovered I could win substantial damages. The advisor was really helpful and guided me through the claim. I knew I had nothing to lose, because of the unique Compensation Claim Protection Plan.

I'd advise anyone who's suffered a personal injury to make that call right now.

Susan Bailey, Croydon

"Claimed £9,560!"

◼ ESTHER SAYS:

I'm glad it worked out well for you, and you got the compensation you deserved for your injury.

As seen on TV

If you've got any further questions about making a claim, I recommend you call FREE NOW

accident advice helpline

Call 0800 0375 375

Call in complete confidence today quoting READ 10

www.aahclaims.com

How to Keep New Year Resolutions

PATRIZIA SAVARESE/CORBIS

MAKING a life change isn't just a matter of raw willpower. These strategies from clinical psychologist Kathleen Cox will help you stick it out:

Really want it How much do you desire change and why? Sometimes it helps to have short-term reasons: effects on your health 30 years down the line can make uninspiring incentives, but if you want to get fit so you can go skiing, this can help you focus.

Plan ahead It's not surprising that you lapse early in January if you impulsively decided on New Year's Day never to smoke or drink again. But if you planned your January detox at the start of December, that mental preparation time can be very helpful.

Be flexible Just because you slip and have a cigarette, it doesn't mean you have to give up trying to quit. Tomorrow's another day.

Get support It's ideal if people can share resolutions. If you want to go to the gym, arrange to go with someone else at set times. On the other hand, if you're trying to give up cigarettes, it won't help to sit next to something who's smoking.

Struggling? To give yourself fresh incentive, try writing a list of pros and cons. Or build a system of rewards for good days.   The Independent

Kissing to the Right

NEXT TIME YOU SNOG, chances are you'll tilt your head to the right, says a recent German study. After spying on kissing couples at airports, stations, beaches and parks in Germany, Turkey and America, Ruhr University psychologist Onur Gunturkun found that 65% tilted right, while 35% went left. (And you thought no one was looking.)

We form the habit in the womb, he says, when foetuses begin to tilt their heads, usually to the right. Most of us then grow to favour the right hand, foot, eye and ear.   SARAH SAFIR

fast fact

1 in 7 British employees would rather **do housework** than attend their office party

Survey for jobs.telegraph.co.uk

A Winner's Guide to Arguing

WHETHER YOU avoid confrontation or go in like a storm trooper, try these tips to boost your persuasive powers:

1. Avoid bad moods. If the other person is in a foul temper you won't get your message across. Just listen for now and find out their grievance.

2. Put yourself in their shoes—arguing with your bosses is bound to make them feel their authority is being undermined. Express yourself in a way they'll be attuned to.

3. If you can plan in advance, write down your three main points. But get the most important across first—you may not get any further.

4. Don't pile on criticism. Raise one issue at a time, constructively.

5. Instead of stating your opinions, try asking questions. You'll show interest—while directing the discussion where you want it to go.

6. Use sympathetic body language. Subtly adopt the same stance as the other person and mimic their gestures (but nothing aggressive). It'll put them more at ease.

7. Discover the other person's real motivation. Your friend complains she never sees you, but the real issue could be jealousy of your new job. Don't waste time arguing over the wrong thing.

Good Housekeeping

Deck the halls . . . and save your marriage

It turns out that Christmas isn't just for children after all. Couples who engage in "meaningful religious holiday rituals", such as dressing the tree, listening to carols or filling the children's stockings, seem less likely to divorce.

Psychologists at Syracuse University, New York, found that couples who placed an emphasis on shared rituals reported a greater "marital satisfaction"—beyond the importance to them of religion in general. Interestingly, men's satisfaction was closely linked to the meaning of rituals, whereas women's was more connected with the routines surrounding them. Such rituals may give couples a chance to share nuances of meaning that affirm their relationship and roles in the family group.

CREATAS

Is Sharing Music Online A Crime?

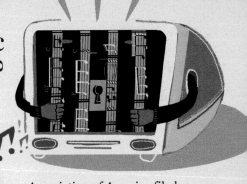

I F IT'S NOT authorised by the owner of the copyright, then yes. "It's stealing, pure and simple," says Sarah Roberts of the British Phonographic Industry. "How would you feel if you created a piece of work only for someone else to take it and offer it free on the Internet?"

This means your children may be breaking the law if they swap music with friends by using software downloaded from sites such as Kazaa, iMesh and Grokster or by e-mailing music files—even if they say "everybody does it."

Record companies are taking the matter so seriously that in the US this year, the Recording Industry Association of America filed lawsuits against 341 members of the public, including a 12-year-old girl who was found to have more than 1,000 copyrighted tracks on her computer hard drive.

Roberts urges music-hungry surfers to visit the growing number of sites with legal downloads (both free and paid for), authorised by the artist, where payments go back to the creator of the music. Visit pro-music.org for more information and links to legal sites.

70% of PC users say they **shout, swear** and are violent to their computer when it **crashes** or goes wrong

MORI

THE PAPERLESS FAX

To receive faxes you need a fax machine that's plugged into a phone socket, turned on, loaded with paper and cleaned regularly. Or you can forget all that. If you've got an Internet connection, uk.efax.com offers a free service that e-mails faxes directly to your computer as image attachments that you print out as and when you please. Download the software and you'll receive an 0870 phone number to give out as your fax number. If you want to send faxes too, you'll need the Efax Plus service which costs £20 a month plus a fee per fax. A similar service is offered at www.pumaone.co.uk.

Calling All Closet Racing Drivers

WHEN IS A PHONE not a phone? When it's being used as a remote control for a small electric car, of course. More and more mobiles are coming with "Bluetooth" capability, the short-range wireless system that is more usually used to share information with a nearby PC or to connect to a wireless headset.

But it looks as if manufacturers are finding other uses for the system—in the future you could be using your phone to control cash machines, your video recorder or the lights in your house.

Sony Ericsson produced this little car as a promotional device for a trade show, but interest has been so high that a limited number are now available to the public, as the CAR-100, for £69.98 (see www. sonyericsson.com). It's only the size of a matchbox, but has an electric motor with two gears. Steering and gear changing can be controlled from the keypad or joystick of a Bluetooth phone from up to ten metres away. It's able to operate without interfering with other devices—so several CAR-100s can be raced against each other.

Get that glow this winter...

WHETHER YOU SEE IT as a fun gimmick or an invaluable way of finding keys (and keyholes) at night, the Glowring X2 is a cheap way of ensuring you're never left in the dark.

Using technology developed for emergency lighting in submarines, this keyfob contains a gas that reacts with a phosphorous coating to produce a constant illumination. It needs no batteries and will glow for ten years. You can attach it to anything you want to find in the dark—bags, zip tags, light pulls, pet collars, even yourself if you want to stand out in a crowd. It comes in three colours and costs £9.99, or £24.99 for three, from www.h3products.com.

Can You Take It Back to the Shop?

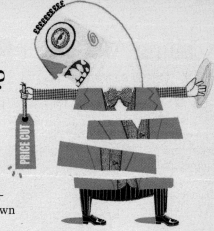

EVERYONE'S TRIED to return a product only for the shop assistant to give some reason why you can't. Were they right?

"We don't give refunds on sale goods." Nonsense. If something is faulty you're entitled to a refund—unless it was specifically marked down because of the fault in question.

"We only give credit notes for unwanted items." If an item's not faulty the shop doesn't have to take it back at all. A credit note's better than nothing.

"You'll have to send it back to the manufacturer." Wrong. Your contract is with the shop so it is legally obliged to take back goods that are faulty.

"We're a franchise." Some chains, such as Snappy Snaps and Thorntons, are franchises, so each shop is a separate business rather than a branch of the same company. Goods from one shop can't be returned to another.

"You have to have a receipt." Wrong. You need proof of purchase but this could be a credit card slip or a bank statement.

Good Housekeeping

Don't let the taxman inherit your money

MANY assume inheritance tax only affects the rich. But soaring house prices mean that many homes are now worth enough to qualify.

Money bequeathed to a spouse or a charity is exempt. Out of what's left, everything over £255,000 is taxed at 40%. You can try giving your assets away while you're alive, but if you

die within seven years those gifts are still taxable. Moreover if the asset is your home and you're still living there,

it's considered still to be yours, and is taxable.

One strategy is to transfer your assets into a trust, either while you're alive or when you die. Spouses who co-own the home can also switch to "tenancy in common", so if one dies their share can be left to descendents, utilising the £255,000 tax free band. See a solicitor or financial planner.

Premier have the *widest* range of Easy Bathing products on the market...

PowerBath
with optional Leg Lift
A comfortable moulded seat with optional leg lift.

FREE AFTERSALES SERVICE

Optional Hydrotherapy
Most popular products in the range come with a hydrotherapy spa option.

Chester
walk-in bath
One of our most popular baths, the Chester has a convenient side entrance, moulded seat and shower

NEW

Walk-In Shower
Our easy-access showers make the most of the smallest spaces

FULLY FITTED

Cambridge
power assisted bath
A normal bath with a walk-in door and power assisted seat.

Belt Lift
Lower gently into your bath with this convenient product.

Easy-Bathe
walk-in bath
The Easy-Bathe combines the luxuries of a bath with the practicalities of a shower and the front opening door allows easy access.

1000's sold around the world

Stratford
compact bath
Our most compact walk-in bath, with all the features you require.

Freephone 0800 018 0088
for details or a free survey

If ringing from outside the uk
Tel: 0044 1527 594215

* Terms and conditions apply. Details available upon request.
Autumn Promotion - October, November & December only.

Please send me a FREE PREMIER COLOUR BROCHURE

Name _____ 3931

Telephone _____

Address _____

_____

_____ Postcode _____

Send to: Premier Bathrooms, FREEPOST BM4591, Redditch, B97 6BR **NO STAMP REQUIRED**

Premier BATHROOMS

Fair Trade is Not Just Coffee

THE IDEA OF GOODS specifically produced without exploiting the Third World people who make them—generally termed "Fair Trade"—is catching on with Western consumers who are happy to pay a bit more for them. And it's not limited to chocolate, tea and coffee.

One Village Sells mostly household goods. You can buy online at www.onevillage.co.uk. The range includes cushions, lampshades, doormats, sandals, gift wrap and even a hammock.

Traidcraft Distributes through independent retailers, listed at www.traidcraft.co.uk, or mail order. Or shop online at store.europe.yahoo. com/fairtradeonline-uk, a joint project with Oxfam, selling games, jewellery, homewares and ornaments. Elephant dung stationery, anyone?

People Tree Offers "organic" clothing, manufactured in a non-polluting way, from a mail order catalogue. Go to www.ptree.co.uk.

Body Shop Not officially Fair Trade, but some ingredients are sourced under a similar scheme. Goods are labelled Community Trade.

TIM BRADLY/GETTY IMAGES

fast fact

82% of senior managers think the UK is vulnerable to an Enron-style **accounting scandal**

MORI

Put a Price on Your Stuff

According to a survey by Primary Direct, 33% of home owners have never calculated the value of their home's contents. But if you are found to be underinsured, then your insurance company has the right to reduce the payout on any claim you make by the same proportion. Fortunately, for £29.50 you can buy a computer program called MyHomeInventory which helps you work it all out. It uses a database (updatable online) to calculate the replacement value of your goods, increases this automatically in line with inflation and even lets you store your inventory online in case your house burns down and you need a record of what was in it. Go to secureinventories.com.

'Margot, the wavy picture on the TV has escaped'

A COLLEAGUE recently confided to me that he had split up with his girlfriend.

I brought him a cup of coffee and lent a sympathetic ear while he complained about his lack of success with the opposite sex.

Finally he asked me: "Why can't I keep a girlfriend?"

As I searched for a sensitive answer, he added, "Is it because I'm married?"

GAVIN BELL, Cambuslang, South Lanarkshire

TO ENTERTAIN a business partner last winter, my father took him to a restaurant in the countryside. They ordered red wine, which arrived ice cold.

"Excuse me," my father's guest gestured to the waitress to tell her, "red wine should be served at room temperature."

"Is that right?" she replied. "Then maybe you should come and visit us again in July." RAMONA RADONICH

I KNEW I was in one of those fancy food shops when I saw the sign over the express lane. Instead of reading "15 items or less", it said, "15 items or *fewer*". JAY RICHARDS

PANICKING WHEN her two-year-old swallowed a tiny magnet, my friend Phyllis rushed him to casualty.

"He'll be fine," the doctor

promised. "The magnet will pass through his system in a day or two."

"How will I be sure?" she pressed.

"Well," the doctor suggested, "you could stick him on the fridge and when he falls off, you'll know."

MARIE THIBODEAU

WHILE QUEUEING in a theme park for a hair-raising ride, I heard my two nephews arguing.

"Aunt Staci's going with me!" insisted Yoni.

"No," said his brother. "She's coming with me!"

Flattered at being so popular, I promised Yoni, "You and I can go on the merry-go-round."

"But I really want you to come on this ride," he protested.

"Why?" I asked.

"Because the more weight there is, the faster it goes."

STACI MARGULIS

HEAVY SNOW had buried my car in our drive. My husband Scott dug around the wheels, rocked the van back and forth and finally pushed me free.

I was on the road when I heard an odd noise so I got on my mobile and called home.

"Thank God you answered," I said when Scott picked up. "There's this sound coming from under the car. For a minute I thought I was dragging you down the motorway."

"And you didn't stop?"

PAIGE FAIRFIELD

£ You could earn £100 for your story. See "It's a Funny Old World" on page 13

166

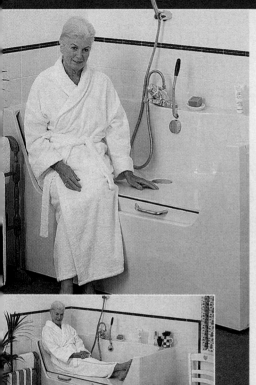

You have just 90 seconds to win at this game! Below we've given you 16 words. Combine each one with another word that starts with the same two letters as that given word. The right answer will create a familiar compound word or two-word phrase. Check out the example, and then see how many you can nail in a minute and a half

Example: Basket _____ball_____

1. Boom _____
2. Secret _____
3. Freeze _____
4. Hot _____
5. Welter _____
6. Sesame _____
7. Touch _____
8. Carrot _____

9. Round _____
10. Common _____
11. Sharp _____
12. Wonder _____
13. Acetic _____
14. French _____
15. Bargain _____
16. Simple _____

Answers: 1. Box 2. Service 3. Frame 4. House 5. Weight 6. Seed 7. Tone 8. Cake 9. Robin 10. Cold 11. Shooter 12. Woman 13. Acid 14. Fries 15. Basement 16. Simon

HOW DO YOU RATE? **14–16** You're cool under pressure! **11–13** Decent. Did the clock get to you? **Below 11** Think about suing your school.

Reader's Digest

LOCAL HEROES

Photographed by
Simon Roberts

Bolton, Greater Manchester
Central heating
engineers Paul
Hudson and Adil
Sarwar used the
tools of their trade
in the face of a
fire—and brought
a child to safety
PAGE 23